PREACHING
FOR
BLACK
SELF-
ESTEEM

PREACHING FOR BLACK SELF-ESTEEM

Emil Thomas
Henry Mitchell

Abingdon Press
Nashville

PREACHING FOR BLACK SELF-ESTEEM

Copyright © 1994 by Abingdon Press

All rights reserved.

This book is printed on recycled, acid-free paper.

ISBN 0-687-33843-3

Unless otherwise noted, scripture quotations are from the King James Version of the Bible.

Scripture quotations marked NIV are taken from the *Holy Bible, New International Version.* Copyright © 1973, 1978, 1984 International Bible Society. Used by permission of Zondervan Publishing House. All rights reserved.

Scripture quotations marked GNB are from the *Good News Bible*—Old Testament: Copyright © American Bible Society 1976; New Testament: Copyright © American Bible Society 1966, 1971, 1976.

Scripture quotations marked TLB are from *The Living Bible* copyright © 1971 by Tyndale House Publishers, Wheaton, IL. Used by permission.

Scripture quotations marked AP are the authors' paraphrase of the Bible.

94 95 96 97 98 99 00 01 02 03 — 10 9 8 7 6 5 4 3 2 1

MANUFACTURED IN THE UNITED STATES OF AMERICA

My work in this book is dedicated to the memory of my father,
Cleave Thomas (1918–1984),
who refused to write Negro *on my birth certificate,*
but instead substituted Ethiopian.

E.T.

To the Second Baptist Church, Columbus, Ohio,
where my Black Self Esteem was nurtured,
and especially to my pastors:
Elbert W. Moore
Charles F. Jenkins

H.M.

Contents

Preface   9

Acknowledgments   11

1. Black Self-Esteem:
   A Vital Need in Search of a Vibrant Ministry   15

2. A History and Theology of Black Self-Esteem   30

3. Self-Esteem and Black Caste:
   Conditions of Birth   42

4. Self-Esteem and Black Characteristics:
   Loving the Way We Look   59

5. Self-Esteem and the Black Continent   77

6. Self-Esteem and Black Capacity   95

7. Self-Esteem and Black Culture   113

8. Self-Esteem and Oppressed Existence   132

9. Preaching for Black Self-Esteem   151

Notes   155

Preface

This pilgrimage to publication began in the late 1970s, when E. K. Bailey of Dallas was inviting Henry H. Mitchell to preach revivals at the Concord Missionary Baptist Church, in connection with Black History Month. Each sermon had to do with some aspect of Black spirituality. The first two revivals were about the biblical affirmations that keep oppressed people alive: "The Theology of Aunt Jane," or "That Ol' Time Religion."

For the next revival, Dr. Bailey raised the widely recognized need for Black self-esteem. The theme "The Spiritual Significance of Black Self-Esteem" was adopted. During that week of services, there was a growing sense that this was the very work of the Holy Spirit. The testimonies that came afterward alerted them to just how relevant this ministry was. It was, in fact, long overdue.

Word spread concerning this revival. Mitchell was invited to repeat it in African American churches from Brooklyn to San Diego. One pastor scheduled it first in Los Angeles, and again when he moved to Baltimore. This theme was repeated over several years.

All the while it was obvious that this focused ministry should be shared in print. Mitchell talked about it, but never sat down to write the book. The excuse was that he was busy, but he had published other books in the meanwhile. In fact, much of this book was already written, in that the messages were already on tape. He assumed that they only needed transcription and editing.

In 1988, when Mitchell visited Jerusalem Baptist Church in Palo Alto, California, he chatted with Pastor Emil Thomas, a good friend and fellow alumnus of Union Theological Seminary. Mitchell had helped in this church's founding, well over forty years before. During the interim, the congregational profile had shifted considerably. Pastor Thomas was struggling with needs peculiar to a middle-class, suburban congregation: self-esteem in the White-ruled worlds of high-tech and finance.

A common bond of interest in self-esteem was formed. Mitchell was delighted to share tapes of his own preaching in the Dallas revivals, where, incidentally, Thomas himself had been active as a Bishop College undergraduate. The tapes helped Thomas get rolling; he soon designed a whole ministry, including the sermons.

The book contains both the Thomas sermons and the ones Mitchell had been holding back. But it is not a book of sermons only. The sermons serve a larger program of Christian growth and maturity, and of healing and wholeness. The focus is on self-esteem. Without sustained ministry in the area of self-esteem, the spiritual wholeness of parishioners is impossible.

It is the prayer of the authors that these pages will be used of God to enrich and strengthen the ministries of African American churches (and others as well), in ways far beyond anyone's fondest dreams. Until recently, those dreams had not even included full consciousness of this grave *spiritual* deficit called low self-esteem. It is time, now, to face the subtle and pervasive heresy of hatred for the human handiwork of God, which is ourselves. African descendants of the first beings made in the image of God can then begin to live up fully to their real potential as the deeply spiritual people they have seemed to be for all these years.

Henry H. Mitchell

Acknowledgments

he completion of this book is the result of the co-operation and support of many. Every audience that ever heard any of the sermons here has helped to refine them. So also has Jerusalem Baptist Church and every professor of Emil Thomas's Doctorate of Ministry Committee at Princeton, and every one of the pastors from coast to coast, when Henry Mitchell preached his revival series on self-esteem at their congregations.

Thanks go also to Martha J. Simmons, independent editorial consultant, who worked closely and tirelessly with both authors to help shape a unified document.

Finally, Alice L. Thomas and Ella P. Mitchell, our wonderful wives, are due the special thanks for the countless extra burdens borne and support given, while husbands added the rigors of writing to their already busy schedules.

PREACHING FOR
BLACK
SELF-
ESTEEM

CHAPTER 1

Black Self-Esteem

A Vital Need in Search of a Vibrant Ministry

"Out of the blackest part of my soul, across the zebra striping of my mind, surges this desire to be suddenly white."[1]

n interesting phenomenon has occurred in Black America at the end of the twentieth century. Any glance at Black youth will reveal a renewal and a renaissance in expressions of ethnic pride. From their fads to their fashions, from their music to their moods, a statement is being made: *"I am an African!"* It is almost a perfect reenactment of our youth culture of the late 1960s to early 1970s. Then processes, "do's," and "conks" gave way to Afros: today Jherri curls have given way to dreadlocks, cornrows, and pictures of Africa carved in one's haircut. Then high-boy shirts and shadow-striped pants were upstaged by dashiki shirts and "tikis" worn about the neck: today casual wear may include leather pendants in red, gold, green and black, and formal wear may utilize Kente cloths from Ghana to adorn tuxedos and evening gowns. Twenty-five years ago the word *Negro* was jettisoned in preference for *Black*; today we are adding to *Black* the term *African American*. Throughout our community, there is a new cultural thrust to celebrate our uniqueness as people of African descent. How can we understand this phenomenon? What are its social precedents? Most important, what need is being addressed in this behavior?

15

Identity Crisis in Black America

Africans in the Americas have long had the confusing task of dealing with a dual identity—that of being both African and American. W. E. B. DuBois, organic intellectual and seminal thinker on the American race question, identified this unique tension in the first half of this century: "One ever feels his two-ness—an American, a Negro; two souls, two thoughts, two unreconciled strivings; two warring ideals in one dark body, whose dogged strength alone keeps it from being torn asunder."[2]

With the exception of Native Americans, the so-called Indians, the Americas are largely inhabited by the descendants of immigrants. After conquering the original inhabitants of the land, Europeans established a nation that was considered a liberal democracy. The population has been largely replenished by more European immigrants, who themselves relinquished much of their ethnic cultures and integrated themselves into the larger Anglo-American society. However, the French, Italians, Germans, and others from the continent could easily solve their crisis of identity by cultural assimilation. By adoption of the English language, Anglo-American cultural mores, economic patterns, and political practices, they could "blend in." Even if the immigrants were slow in this regard, their children could easily accomplish the same. And if all failed, they could marry with other Americans—after all, they *were* "White."

For people of color, however, the prospect of assimilation and therefore acceptance into mainstream American society has proved difficult at best and impossible at worst. The Europeans who colonized this country brought with them a legacy of racism that was woven into the warp and woof of the society. Hundreds of years of chattel slavery were not easily erased by emancipation in the 1860s. Laws of segregation prevented the freed, but largely uneducated, slaves from receiving an equal education. Economic oppression and political disenfranchisement were basic facts of life for descendants of Africans a century after the abolition of slavery. As if that were not enough, they were ostracized, demonized, and perpetually lampooned by a society that glorified whiteness while justifying these blatant social inequities. European immigrants had a distinct advantage—they had light skin in a land that worshiped all that was European. Brown skin, tightly curled hair, and West African features prevented other people from ever being viewed with favor by the ruling race.

Black people were perpetually reminded that they were different. Because of systematic restriction from access to African history, they knew precious little of their past. With such historical and social alienation from Africa, the vast majority of Black people had little option but to see themselves as Americans. In a sense, since the only history most of them knew was American history, they were perhaps more American than everyone else, save perhaps, the Native Americans! Therefore, the crisis of identity was a peculiar tension for African Americans, who had little contact with or knowledge of their African roots, but had ample evidence that they were not fully accepted in American society because of their blackness.

Two Major Responses: Integrationist and Nationalist

The history, culture, politics, and psychology of African Americans reveal two primary modes of response to this duality of identity: integrationism and nationalism. Generally speaking, the integrationist seeks to resolve the identity crisis by emphasizing the American side of Black identity. An integrationist will highlight the Black presence in American history, celebrate Black contributions to American culture, and advocate inclusion and participation of Blacks in American society. Psychologically, integrationists consider themselves Americans who happen to be Black. On the other hand, nationalists emphasize the African side of Black identity. A nationalist will highlight African history, celebrate African culture, and advocate participation in the development of the Black community in America and Africa. Psychologically, nationalists consider themselves Africans who happen to be Americans.

The interplay of integrationist and nationalist perspectives of Black identity has ranged from creative cooperation to polar opposition. In the twentieth century, the disparate positions of Black integrationist and nationalist leaders have often been magnified in the media—as if to portray Black disunity. The fact is that deep ideological differences did and do exist in the visions of an integrationist like W. E. B. DuBois and a nationalist like Marcus Garvey, or integrationist Martin Luther King, Jr. and nationalist Malcolm X, or integrationist Jesse Jackson and nationalist Louis Farrakhan. There are also extremes in both perspectives. On the extreme wing of integrationists are the assimilationists, who reject their African heritage, identifying themselves simply as "humans." On the extreme wing of the nationalists are the separatists, who deny their American influences, identifying themselves exclusively as Africans.

As different as these positions may be, the gap between integrationist and nationalist perspectives is narrowing rather than widening. As the twentieth century moves toward its end, integrationist and nationalist leaders are moving closer to one another in positions, in perspectives, and in partnerships. Whereas W. E. B. DuBois and Marcus Garvey were scathing and bitter critics of each other, Martin Luther King, Jr. and Malcolm X had a civil personal meeting, and each privately admired the other's work. In more recent times, Jesse Jackson and Louis Farrakhan worked together in a presidential campaign until politically inexpedient, and even then continued to maintain a personal friendship. The mood of the Black masses, while favoring integrationism, has never exclusively embraced one perspective or the other, but has swung like a pendulum from one pole to the other, depending on the tone and tenor of the times.

Black Identity After the Civil Rights Era

The Civil Rights Era of the 1950s and 1960s allowed questions of Black identity to be thoroughly explored in the African American community. From the midfifties to the midsixties, the prevailing perspective was that of the integrationist. Charismatic ministers and civil rights leaders like Martin Luther King, Jr.,

Ralph Abernathy, Ella Baker, Wyatt T. Walker, and Andrew Young led an army of courageous Christians across the South in a nonviolent war to tear down the bastions of segregation in America—yet they did more than win social, legal, and political victories. They liberated the Black psyche and pricked the White conscience. As visible examples of Black excellence in educational preparation, moral stature, political wisdom, and courageous Christian militancy, millions of their Black brothers and sisters took new pride in themselves as integral members of the American society and viable players on the political scene. This defiance of White dominance spurred the shedding of a corporate inferiority complex. Additionally, some White people were ashamed to see that such exemplary American citizens were being beaten and abused lawfully in "the land of the free and the home of the brave." Black churches swelled with young men and women who saw the Christian movement as much an advocate of saved souls as a vanguard for the liberation of the oppressed.

However, in the midsixties, cries of "Black Power" were heard on the fringes of the movement. A crowd of younger students in the Student Non-Violent Coordinating Committee (SNCC), led by persons like the Trinidad-born and Howard University-educated Stokely Carmichael, began to push for Black people to accomplish goals that did not involve the wider American society. These voices sounded more like those of nationalists, like the apocalyptic Elijah Muhammad or Pan-Africanist Malcolm X, than the dream of Martin Luther King, Jr. Northern, urbanized Blacks recognized that the right to sit next to a White person on a toilet in public bathrooms was not enough to undo centuries of systematic alienation from their African history and heritage. For the first time, African culture became widely popular among Black people, as evidenced in their Afros, dashikis, and even in the naming of some of their children.

Integration and the Black Community

After the sudden and tragic deaths of Malcolm X and Martin Luther King, Jr., American society officially and legally adopted elements of the vision of integration. Schools were integrated by forced busing. White neighborhoods were opened to Black residents. Affirmative Action programs were implemented to remedy hundreds of years of subjugation and legal segregation. In an unprecedented measure, large segments of the African American population gained access to the institutions of the larger society— this time not only as servants and functionaries, but as beneficiaries. Gradually, more and more Black people attended White schools, lived in White neighborhoods, and joined White organizations. A new Black middle class emerged. Previously, the Black middle class was largely populated by professionals, artisans, and tradespeople who served their own community. However, in the 1970s and 1980s, a new climate emerged in which Black teachers could teach White students, Black physicians could treat White patients, and Black lawyers could have White clients.

The legacy of integration of the 1970s and 1980s had a devastating social and psychological effect on the African American community at large. First, integration effected a devastating and deleterious "brain-drain" on the Black community, depleting historically Black neighborhoods and institutions of many of their brightest and best. Large numbers of the Black middle class, including the indigenous intelligentsia, relocated to the suburbs, and marshaled their skills to the service of largely White communities, businesses, and institutions. Though there were immediate economic benefits for these individual members and families of this talented Black middle class, the communities that were left behind were robbed of their upwardly mobile brothers and sisters. DuBois' vision of the talented tenth was reversed: ironically, the "talented tenth" of the African American crop was no longer linked and locked into service and leadership of their own community—but was harnessed rather for the development of wealth among the rulers of White America. The boon and benefit for America in general was a curse for the Black community in particular. Urban communities, uncharacteristically devoid of some of their brightest products, began a downward spiral of self-destruction. Black institutions experienced unprecedented deterioration. The Black family fragmented, as single parenthood became as common as the traditional two-family homes. Some Black colleges struggled, while others closed. Black neighborhoods were plagued by drugs and violence, and public schools reflected the problems of the community. Integration had provided access to the larger society for some individuals, but it had been at the expense of an eroding Black community.

Self-Esteem, Suburbia, and Black Identity

Integration also exacted a price from those who were integrated. While the upwardly mobile Black middle class appeared outwardly successful, they experienced an inward psychic struggle. Existence in the White enclaves of suburbia exposed them to new affronts and attacks on their self-esteem. Whereas before desegregation, Black people were forced to live in neighborhoods populated by a majority of their own race, integration often sprinkled Black families in a largely White world. Leaving the limitations of the ghetto also meant leaving their own community, a realm within the larger society where Black culture, religion, and politics reigned supreme. In the suburbs, Black music, art, and aesthetics were considered quaint. In the Black community, the achievements and excellence of African Americans were admired, respected, and rewarded. In the suburbs, Black people were not often those to receive the recognition and awards that they might have received in their own community. In the Black community leadership was recruited, cultivated, and exalted. In the suburbs, Black students were rarely selected for class president, the debate team, or "Who's Who." Many were channeled into sports, or worse yet, some were placed in special education early on, because they were viewed as "hyperactive." The self-esteem of Black male students suffered disproportionately in the classes of White female teachers. In traditional Black churches, Black people served in a plethora of leadership roles, as trustees, stewards, deacons, missionaries, and so on. However, when they joined the "integrated" churches, they were seldom selected for positions of authority and influence, but often ended up in the choir stand, as the gushing congregation remarked about how "they sing so well." In short, the suburbs often revealed that White Americans still considered the descendants of Africa as a lesser breed.

This phenomenon wreaked havoc on the psychology and spirituality of some who had left their communities in search of "a better life." The ensuing problem was a deficit in ethnic self-esteem. This is not to say that the upwardly mobile Black people who had infiltrated White America had no pride. Quite the contrary, they continued to be proud of the many accomplishments in their lives. Many were proud of their education, economic status, their homes, their moral rectitude, and of their families in general. And many were proud of their personal spirituality, manifesting the aristocratic air of those who "know that they know that they know that they're saved." However, in pursuit of the dream of an integrated society, some had deemphasized or discarded altogether their ethnic identity, and the joy of being who they were.

The Symptoms of Low Ethnic Self-Esteem

How does one evaluate low self-esteem as it relates to one's race?[3] There is little research or literature generally available on the impact of racism on psychological health or spiritual wholeness. In order to focus a ministry that will seek healing and wholeness for those who may not esteem that aspect of the self that identifies one with a particular racial group, five axes are identified under which issues of racial self-esteem may be examined.

Axis I: Black Caste. To be born Black in America is to be born under the insignia of inferiority. Historically speaking, in American society, Blackness is considered something to be overcome or transcended. Dark skin does not give one any particular advantages in this country. Quite the contrary, the dominant culture is constantly suspicious of Black people. Persons with black skin are assumed to come from a caste of people who are lacking in economic clout, intellectual ability, and moral rectitude. On the other hand, those persons who have white skin are more often assumed to be financially sound, mentally astute, and morally pure. If you come from the Black caste, you must prove that you are not poor, dumb, and criminal, or else it will be assumed. If you are from the White caste, if you do not prove that you are not financially secure, smarter than average, or virtuous, it will often be assumed. Dark skin and African features are given less credit in this country.

Caste, the social status prescribed for people at birth because of the group to which they were born, causes not a few African Americans to seek escape from the stigmas of their origins. It can be seen in people who conveniently hide their small-town roots, single-parent families, or poor backgrounds. It can be seen in attempts to override the lower caste of color with excessive aquisitions of social status symbols like clothes, cars, and credit cards. It may explain the exodus of some of the Black middle class from inner-city communities, in which they were nurtured, for the status of the suburbs. It may even be a factor for some of the people who change their names from their given names once they reach adulthood. Sometimes the quest for "class" is an attempt to escape the shame of caste.

Axis II: Black Characteristics. There is a tendency among some Black Americans to deemphasize, modify, or attempt to escape altogether some of the physical features and characteristics that identify their African ancestry. Some children and youth express their desire for "straight" hair in preference for their own "nappy" hair, which is devalued as "bad" hair. Some young adults have opted for blue, gray, or green contact lenses over their own naturally brown eyes. Other adults at times dye their hair blond, red, or even blue, or have sported wigs of these various hues—when their own hair is naturally brown or black. Some men chemically treat their hair, "relaxing" the tightness and toughness of its natural texture to achieve the effect known as a "curl." Some of the most popular and visible Black entertainers utilize some of these techniques.

Certainly people of all cultures recognize the value of cosmetics in enhancing one's features. However, the above-mentioned practices have the effect of making one appear to be less African and more European. Why is it that White characteristics are the ones that are chosen when some Black people seek to enhance their features cosmetically? Is it because physical characteristics that are common to Whites are considered more beautiful than those common to Black people? When the purpose of cosmetics is for the express purpose of making one escape one's own genetic heritage, this is a clear rejection of one's self.

Axis III: Black Continent. Every ethnic group in the United States with a healthy sense of self points proudly to a homeland, a country of origin. These geographical "roots" serve as symbols of great histories and glorious accomplishments. However, the institution of slavery and the Eurocentric education of the Americas have systematically denied Black people this benefit. Consequently, there is often little or no sense of affinity or affection for Africa as the homeland in the minds and hearts of many Black people. Sadly, significant numbers of Black Americans have internalized images and notions of Africa that are negative.

There is little teaching or preaching in Black churches on African history. Large portions of the Bible refer to Egypt, and numerous references are included about Ethiopia, Libya, "The Queen of the South," and so on. However, based upon the virtual absence of these texts in sermons and Sunday schools, they are not generally seen as significant to African Americans. The majority of Christian clergy and educators simply don't study or evaluate the relevance of these scriptures to the Black community. To reject a positive identification with Africa, the continent of origin of the ancestors of Black Americans, is to reject a portion of one's own origins and history, and a significant part of oneself.

Axis IV: Black Capacity. Black people have achieved glorious accomplishments in the sciences, medicine, mathematics, politics, and in every field of human endeavor. However, the larger American society has craftily communicated that Black people are good at some things, and bad at others. For example, media and literature are filled with messages and images of Black competence as entertainers in sports, music, and the arts. Sadly, however, images of Black entrepreneurs, scientists, scholars, and leaders are all too few.

These messages are internalized not only by the dominant society, but in the Black psyche. It can be seen when African Americans express unwarranted suspicion of the services of Black professionals. It can be seen in persons who resent the images of the *Cosby Show* as being literally impossible for Black people. It can be seen in the passion of children who dream of being a basketball star like Magic Johnson or a boxer like Mike Tyson, but can't dream of being a military genius like General Colin Powell or a scientist and astronaut like Dr. Mae Jemison. Something is wrong when people believe that they must be more physically talented than mentally gifted. That something is a lack of confidence in Black capacity, a clear deficit in self-esteem.

Axis V: Black Culture. Black people in this country have created a beautiful culture, a complex of art, language, values, and religion that is authentically African, yet uniquely American. Whether it involves "playing the dozens" with the boys on the block, playing "double-dutch" with the girls in the hood, cooking gumbo, or shouting down the aisles in church on Sunday, there is a distinct cultural difference between Black and White Americans.

However, there are some who make a conscious effort to sift out all of the cultural components etched into their consciousness by nature and nurture. Some people overcompensate in pronunciation, seemingly attempting to sound out words more precisely than their White counterparts, because they consider Black English "bad" English. Others would not be caught dead in a church that involved ecstatic experiences with the Spirit of God, because they consider such behavior to be "ignorant." There are even those who refuse to listen to blues, jazz, or rap music, because it is "uncultured." We must clearly recognize that the African Diaspora is rich in diversity, so rich that any discussion of "who's Blacker than who" is culturally preposterous and politically absurd. However, when individuals make desperate attempts to wash out any vestiges of Black culture from their lives, we must at least consider that such a person is ashamed of that same culture.

This list of axes is not by any means exhaustive of the causes or symptoms of low ethnic self-esteem in any given context or community. However, in spite of the fact (perhaps *because* of the fact) that African Americans are moving into the realm of the White middle class, social and cultural assimilation has highlighted these issues as a unique problem. These examples also provide a manageable starting point for any church's ministry to low ethnic self-esteem.

Self-Esteem, Survival, and the Love Ethic of Jesus

A rationale for ministry is not complete with a review of history and analysis of a need. For a ministry to have integrity, it must be clinically defensible and biblically justifiable. In other words, self-esteem itself must be defined in light of the insights of relevant psychological literature as well as the mandate of the Scriptures. A sound definition of self-esteem that is rooted in the Holy Scriptures can only enhance the traditional role of the Black church as a guarantor of the survival of Black people in America.

Self-Esteem: Definitions and Delineations

Self-esteem is an issue that is rapidly gaining interest these days. From the proposals of educators to include self-esteem–building material into public school curricula, to the rhetorical litanies of Jesse Jackson proclaiming "I am Somebody!", self-esteem is a topic that is engendering wider acceptance as essential for human wholeness. However, what is often lost in our educational objectives and our pulpit pronouncements is a clear definition of self-esteem that is intellectually defensible and clinically justifiable.

> By self-esteem we refer to the evaluation which the individual makes and customarily maintains with regard to [himself]: it expresses an attitude of approval or disapproval, and indicates the extent to which the individual believes [himself] to be capable, significant, successful, and worthy. In short, self-esteem is a personal judgment of worthiness that is expressed in the attitudes the individual holds toward [himself]. It is a

subjective experience which is conveyed to others by verbal reports and other expressive behavior.[4]

Psychologist Stanley Coopersmith describes four primary sources of self-esteem: capability, significance, success, and worthiness. The scope of this book concerns the relevance of ethnicity to self-esteem, which would fall under the category of what Coopersmith calls *significance*, "the acceptance, attention, and affection of others."[5] If the acceptance, affection, and attention of others is an antecedent to our own acceptance, affection, and attention to our own selves, and if our race impacts the nature of the acceptance, affection, and attention of others, then race will impact our sense of significance.

Ethnic self-esteem is the enduring evaluation that one makes about the significance of one's race, culture, and history as attributes of oneself.

Survival, Self-Love, and Salvation

At least one element of the genius of Black people is the tenacious ability to survive in a hostile environment. The many and various modes of struggle of the descendants of Africans in the West have often incorporated unusual adaptability and flexibility, with a high priority on the sacredness of survival. During slavery, Black people were living witnesses of the wisdom of the Bible, which states, "To every thing there is a season, and a time to every purpose under the heaven" (Eccles. 3:1). There were times of work to satisfy the master's desire for productivity. There were times of playing and dancing to release the tension of pent-up psychic pain. There were times of worship to sustain the soul. There were times to escape to freedom. There were times to rebel. And there were also times of prudential acquiescence to survive to another day. After slavery, Black people gradually spread across the land, from Juneau to Jacksonville, from Hoboken to Honolulu. However, because of the reality of racism, different methodologies of survival evolved in different contexts in order to ensure survival as a people. Accordingly, the ministry of the Black church has been based upon a theology of survival. While the White cultural emphasis on individual success has characterized the ministry of the White church, the Black contextual emphasis on corporate survival and liberation have characterized the ministry of the Black church.

So as not to be totally captivated by culture or context, it is essential that a ministry of ethnic self-esteem within the Black church be rooted in the Scriptures, if it is to issue forth in existential and eternal survival. A ministry of self-esteem is wholly compatible with the Love Ethic of Jesus Christ. In responding to the query of a scribe who desired to know Jesus' perspective on the greatest commandment, Jesus responded with the two greatest commandments, quoting Deuteronomy 6:5, and Leviticus 19:18, respectively:

> "The most important one," answered Jesus, "is this: 'Hear O Israel, the Lord our God, the Lord is one. Love the Lord your God with all your heart and with all your soul and with all your mind and with all your strength.' The second is this: 'Love your neighbor as yourself.' There is no commandment greater than these." (Mark 12:29-31 NIV)

Included and incorporated with the love of God and the love of the neighbor is the love of the self. In the mind of Jesus, the three were so intertwined and intermeshed that he included them in his answer to the scribe. A closer look at Leviticus 19:18 reveals an almost symbiotic relationship between love of one's self and love of one's neighbor: self-love is the pattern and paradigm for neighbor-love. Also, love of the self is *assumed.* "Love your neighbor as yourself " implies that the lover is already loved—at least by himself or herself! A theology of Black self-esteem will be discussed more fully in the next chapter.

One of the assumptions of this book is that *Black people have learned how not to love themselves.* Living in a racist society that denigrates Blackness and deifies Whiteness is not healthy for those of the darker hue. Living in the midst of a system based upon notions of White supremacy is not only an affront to human dignity, but it is also a constant strain on the psyche, which must be addressed anew in each generation. If Coopersmith's formulation is correct in stating that one believes oneself to be *significant* to the extent that he or she receives the affection, attention, or concern of another, then the West is guilty of committing an awesome crime against Black folk and others in teaching that to be other than White is to be less than human. This teaching is abundant today in schools where children are taught that the pharaohs were White and that ancient Egypt was more European than it was African. It is taught every time a situation comedy emerges with a White hero with a Black sidekick, whether the hero be Jack Benny, Robert Urich, or Tom Selleck. This learning process can cause dissonance in the consciousness of the young before they are old enough to critique such messages. James Cone expresses the loss of a sense of *significance* in existential terms as the loss of *meaning* as it relates to one's blackness:

> It is not that the black man is absurd or that the white society as such is absurd. Absurdity arises as the black man seeks to understand his place in the white world. The black man does not view himself as absurd; he views himself as human. But as he meets the white world and its values, he is confronted with an almighty No and is defined as a thing. This produces the absurdity.[6]

This book is a ministry that will seek to "unlearn" the racist messages that are communicated to Black people in this society, while enhancing the ethnic self-esteem of African Americans, in the pursuit of a holy and holistic self-love.

The thesis of this book is that self-esteem can be positively effected when the following occurs: (1) people receive more information about themselves, and (2) people begin to appropriately celebrate their God-given worth. The sermons presented herein are examples of biblical information prepared with the dual goals of providing information and inspiration. The discussion questions included with the sermons are examples of questions that can be raised in discussion groups with those who have shared in the sermon event.

The intended result of this ministry is that African American Christians will (1) understand their ethnicity as meaningful rather than meaningless, (2) view their racial identity with greater appreciation, and (3) perceive their ethnic identity and heritage as worthy of celebration, praise, and gratitude to God.

CHAPTER 2

A History and Theology of Black Self-Esteem

A deep belief in self-worth cannot be sustained solely by surface concerns. Even the United States Constitution and its amendments are not sufficient. Profound self-respect has to have deeper foundations. A Bible-based theology or doctrine has already been suggested. It is now time to look in greater detail at this doctrine, so powerful yet so often unspoken. It is time to consider the historic roots and impressive arguments for the idea that "I am somebody." With deep awareness of these roots and religious foundations, self-esteem will not easily be shaken—not by the assaults of the majority culture or the hardships of experience at the bottom or any other influence.

Self-Esteem in Black History

Our ancestors did not leave the shores of Africa with low self-esteem. Their traditional culture and religion had been supportive of selfhood in many ways, both in belief and in direct experience. Unlike some Eastern religions, African Traditional Religion (ATR) contained no notions of a divinely ordained permanent underclass or caste. Even slavery, in Africa, was a temporary fact born of debt or defeat in battle. The first generations of enslaved Africans in America viewed slavery much the same way. Self-esteem was supported in ATR by a belief system and by many folk customs.

African children were and are held in awe because all are believed to have conferred on them a specific personhood or character just before their souls leave heaven to be born on earth. This unique aspect of each person is called the *ori* by the Yoruba and the *kra* by the Ashanti. To seek to interfere with this *ori* or *kra* that God made in each child could stir divine wrath. In addition to this, each child was and is believed to be an extension of the line by which his or her ancestors continue to live. It is thus easy to see why and how children are adored and indulged in their formative years.

Despite all the oppression endured by African Americans right up to the present, this tendency to adore and indulge babies persists. Long years of unthinkable oppression in the rural South and urban America have begun to erode this tradition of loving children into a healthy start toward self-esteem. But even without the belief systems of the *ori* and the *kra*, the tradition of deep care for children lives on in some of Black America. It is still odd for an orphaned or abandoned child in some Black communities not to be informally adopted into some family, regardless of kinship.

Another folkway that subtly supports self-esteem is found in the awe, respect, and permissiveness with which people are received when possessed by the Holy Spirit ("shout") in public worship. This dates back to similar African acceptance of those possessed by the subdeities of ATR. The Spirit also leads soloists to render their own personal versions of songs. The applause that follows these creative improvisations is the highest possible type of support for self-esteem. Whether shouting or singing, the African American worshiper is affirmed and esteemed to the highest.

These roots in African beliefs and customs provided the self-esteem needed for slaves to keep their sanity, and even to wax creative with revolts for their liberation. It took a long time for these African self-esteem influences to die out. In fact, the lowest period of Black self-esteem and discouragement was likely not during slavery. It was probably the late 1800s through the early

1900s. During slavery Blacks still proudly named whole denominations "*African* Methodist" (1816 and 1820) and called local churches "First *African*" Presbyterian or Baptist church.

Prior to the Civil War, the most impressive evidence of slave dignity and self-respect was the spiritual. Hundreds had liberation as their main theme. Behind the plaintive cries of song after song, towering strength of character was evident. In the spiritual "Oh Freedom" one hears a disguised paean of self-respect: "And before I'd be a slave, / I'd be buried in my grave." The part about going home to God and being free was part of the disguise. They were declaring the freedom of their minds already.

African Americans learned to be ashamed of themselves as African after the close of the Reconstruction era. When the federal troops were withdrawn from the seceded states in 1878, ex-slaves were subjected to limitless mob violence. Regardless of the amendments to the federal Constitution, they now had no rights that a White was bound to respect. This living in constant terror understandably undermined the self-confidence of many, many Blacks. They also learned from their White teacher-friends to admire the culture of Whites more than they respected their own. Without the hundreds of teachers who poured South to teach the ex-slaves to read and write, emancipation would have been meaningless. But this indispensable training was a mixed blessing. Often without intent on the teachers' part, this education implied, nevertheless, that everything Black was inferior. "The White man's ice was colder," and so on. As we have seen, this attitude is prevalent even today.

The influence of White Christian *beliefs* on self-esteem has also been mentioned—some naturally good, some actually bad. Christian faith supported African culture when based in church-family communities. Christian faith encouraged African moral character and joy in hard work. But the favorite hymn (composed by a White) of Blacks referred to the singer as a wretch: "Amazing Grace" that "saved a wretch like me." Another hymn asked, "Would he devote that sacred head for such a worm as I?" These theological ideas penetrated deeply when sung so often and so fervently.

Thus, despite good influences, any assessment of Christian orthodoxy's influence must acknowledge its belief that all human beings are depraved, even totally depraved, apart from grace. Isaiah 64:6 refers to all our righteousnesses as filthy rags. And the apostle Paul cries out in Romans 7:24, "O wretched man that I am! who shall deliver me from the body of this death?" Although Jesus himself made no such sweeping appraisal of human nature, these ideas are in the Bible and in the corpus of Christian belief.

For the oppressed, such a doctrine becomes a means of continued "put-down." Historically, African Americans have ill afforded such a depressive in a world where they were already put down too far. Depravity of any degree is only a small part of the total Bible statement. And every doctrine must bear the test of *all* the Bible.

The Biblical/Theological Basis of Self-Esteem

In Genesis 1:26-27 there is unequivocal testimony: "So God said, Let us make humankind in our own image" (AP). In the image of God they were created; male and female. For the oppressed and the depressed, this is the kind of healing word and emphasis that is required. And this sort of nourishment for the crushed spirit can be found throughout the Bible.

The psalmist (8:3-4) sang out, "When I consider thy heavens, the work of thy fingers, the moon and the stars, which thou hast ordained; What is man, that thou art mindful of him? and the son of man, that thou visitest him?" Again from the psalms (139:14) comes that great affirmation of personhood: "I will praise thee; for I am fearfully and wonderfully made: marvelous are thy works; and that my soul knoweth right well."

The entire ministry of Jesus was devoted to the liberation, healing, and affirming of people who had both low social status and low self-esteem. After a Syrophoenecian woman (a "foreigner") expressed esteem for herself at the level of a dog, Jesus affirmed her to the highest, saying, "O woman, great is thy faith: be it unto thee even as thou wilt" (Matt. 15:28). When a woman in cultural quarantine (put down and isolated for having hemorrhages) cringed with fear after touching the hem of his garment, Jesus assured her also (Luke 8:43-48). When a common thief hanging on a cross humbly asked to be remembered, Jesus promised him a place in paradise (Luke 23:43). And the Gospel of John records (14:12) that he carefully raised the self-confidence of his discouraged disciples to the highest. He crowned his own ministry with the promise that they would do even greater work than he had done.

Even the apostle Paul, author of so much about the human spirit that seems negative, had reassuring things to say from time to time. He told the Thessalonians to encourage the fainthearted, help the weak, and be patient with everybody (I Thess. 5:14). He told young Timothy not to let anyone despise him just because he was young (I Tim. 4:12). He went on then to advise him that he was perfectly capable of being an example to all, regardless of age.

Paul had so much confidence in Timothy that he sent him to Corinth, his most troublesome church. Paul then wrote to the Corinthians (16:10-12) to request their support and encouragement of young Timothy. In his second letter to Timothy, Paul advised him to stir up the gifts (talents) God had given him. His final word in that connection was perhaps the most powerfully supportive word for self-esteem in the entire Bible: "God hath not given us the spirit of fear; but of power, and of love, and of a sound mind" (II Tim. 1:7).

The most widely familiar text on self-esteem in all of the New Testament (mentioned in chapter 1), however, does not state the point directly. "Thou shalt love thy neighbour *as thyself*." This portion of the summary of the Law is found in Matthew 19:19 and 22:9; Mark 12:31, and Luke 10:27. Whether stated by Jesus or someone else, however, it was quoted from the book of Leviticus, 19:18. In other words, it was no new idea even in Jesus' day; it was part of the original Law. It had been taken for granted very early that one ought to love or accept oneself. The love of neighbor could not be less than or more than the love and acceptance of self: "*as* thyself."

This ancient, holy, folk wisdom was reflected or implicit in other passages. Jesus' model prayer asks God for forgiveness "*as* we forgive our debtors" (Matt. 6:12). And this principle is applied in the parable of the unmerciful servant (Matt. 18:21-35). Here the servant who was forgiven a huge debt sees the mercy extended him revoked. This is in keeping with the mercy he failed to extend to his fellow servant. All of this reminds one of a clinical fact: those who do not forgive others have not been able themselves to accept the forgiveness of God. And just as forgiveness of self is conditional upon the forgiveness of others, so is real love and acceptance of self conditional upon the love extended to others.

The importance of this parallel was not apparent, however, in ancient Israel. It was Jesus himself who first linked this law of love for neighbors (Lev. 19:18) to the very love of God (Deut. 6:5). Jesus' New Testament summary places love of neighbor alongside the love of God, which is to be with "all thine heart, and with all thy soul, and with all thy might." The importance here attached to the love of neighbor is thus inescapably assigned also to the love of self. Given the fact that love of God is the most important, love of self (and of neighbor) is far more significant both biblically and clinically than most devout Christians tend to be aware.

Responses to Challenges

The question then arises as to how so significant a principle could escape common notice for so long. Passages from the Bible and common hymns that view humans as depraved have already been mentioned. But it may be that the misinterpretation of a word from Jesus himself has done more to destroy self-esteem in the modern mind than any of these.

It is Jesus' requirement that to follow him one must *deny* oneself (Matt. 16:24; Mark 8:34; Luke 9:23). Whether consciously or unconsciously, typically sincere Christians sense a contradiction between this *self-denial* and the *self-affirmation* proposed here. For them, the self-affirmation in Jesus' summary of the Law is only implied, at best; maybe not even that. Certainly the love of self is not declared with force equal to the requirement of self-denial. How then does one resolve this apparent contradiction?

The resolution hinges on careful translation/interpretation of the original words for deny and love. Both words are prone to connote narrow and inadequate meanings as they are encountered in virtually all the common translations of the New Testament.

The Living Bible offers some clues, however. Mark 8:34 is translated, "If any of you wants to be my follower, you must put aside your own pleasures and shoulder your cross, and follow me closely." The Greek word which is translated as "deny" by so many can mean forgetting one's self, or losing sight of one's own personal interests. In other words, the denial is not an utter put-down of one's total personhood. It is not self-martyrdom. It is, rather, a refusal to be controlled by one's lesser pleasures and self-centered interests—a refusal to let lower goals and lesser priorities crowd out the larger concerns of the kingdom of God. It is in these concerns or "crosses" that one finds complete fulfillment. This is the highest form of self-affirmation.

This interpretation of *self-denial* is fully and immediately justified by the verse that follows the denial verse in all three Gospels. "For whosoever will save his life shall lose it; and whosoever shall lose his life for my sake and the gospel's, the same shall *save* it" (Mark 8:35). The denial required is obviously applied to the lesser concerns and more selfish interests of less than mature believers. Once again Jesus is clinically verifiable: self-centeredness is far from self-fulfilling. In fact, one loses real life and living when self is the center of one's world.

So self-denial is not self-crucifixion. It is the careful pruning away of lower goals and lesser priorities. Self-denial is the liberating refusal to let lesser ends crowd out the greater and more truly fulfilling goals in life.

Jesus, who came to bring abundant life (John 10:10), insists that one *finds* that abundant life by giving one's own best self with reckless abandon. And this is, paradoxically, the very affirmation of self that the passage seemed on the surface to deny. The resolution of the apparent contradiction is easy when one distinguishes between the self-centered self and the self who is made in the very image of God. This self is joyously, abundantly fulfilled in giving.

The other theoretical source of resistance to "self-love" or self-esteem and affirmation is this word *love*. Again, the answer lies in distinguishing between the Greek meanings that are translated as "love" in English. The most common connotations of love as applied to the self are unfortunately self-centered, or narcissistic. Self-love of this type is a grievous sin that can in fact lead to a form of mental illness.

The "agape" love of the New Testament is quite the opposite of self-centered love. It is all too often applied to everybody except the self. Yet it applies as much to persons themselves as to neighbors and God. This is a love that, quite literally in Greek, wishes persons well, or desires the welfare of others.

Agape comes from God (I John 4:7), in the sense that persons can rise to the level of self-giving love only after they have accepted enough of God's love to feel secure in giving. That love and acceptance from God first makes a person lovable or acceptable to herself or himself. Thus the love of self is possible because of the love of God; to accept it is to love and accept the self *and* others in response. It may sound trite to some, but it is literally true: "We love God because God first loved us" (I John 4:19 AP).

So the love of God and neighbor and self are all inextricably bound together. Jesus placed them together for good cause. And anyone who seeks to separate them, or to achieve one without the other, is attempting the impossible. As I John 4:20-21 clearly states, it is impossible to love God and hate one's brother. And what can be said of the brother can also be said of the self.

Not only are God, neighbor, and self inseparable biblically, they are inseparable clinically. Psychologists know well the impossibility of sound, healthy self-love without love for others and without love for the Giver of all love. In effect, without self-esteem or healthy self-love, it is impossible to love anyone else or to love

God. Healthy, positive self-acceptance or love is not a modern fad or intellectual insight; it is the very will of God for each and every one of God's children.

Dealing with Extremes

Every doctrine has a way of being taken to extremes at times, and of generating or being responded to by opposite extremes. The doctrine of healthy self-esteem begets extremes in its own direction and extremes in opposite reaction. Those who have Bible-based and spiritually affirmed self-acceptance face two major challenges. One is avoiding erroneous extremes of their own, and the other is charitably and open-mindedly dealing with opposing extremes.

With certitude of belief in the self fully documented in the Bible, one could go to extremes of self-righteousness. The more likely danger, however, is that of a cult of humanism with less and less awareness of God. When Jesus said that the sabbath was made for people, and not people for the sabbath (Mark 2:27), he clearly established that religious observance was made for the benefit of human beings. In other words, humankind is at the center of creation, and God doesn't need Sabbath observance; *we* do. The self-esteem of human beings is wise and healthy only in the context of a world where God is still Lord of the Sabbath and everything else. As quoted above (Ps. 139:14), human beings are "fearfully and wonderfully made." But made by whom and for what? The beauty and glory of humanity fades fast when it drifts from the will of its Creator. So self-esteem is valid only because it is the will of the Creator. It is not because human beings are independently of supreme worth. That worth is fixed by God. The Shorter Cathechism of the Presbyterians correctly said that the chief end of human beings is to glorify God (not self), and enjoy God forever.

Certitude about the self can also breed static, doctrinaire rigidity—hidebound opposition to the faith of others. However, this rule of the inseparability of love of God, neighbor, and self applies in very dynamic ways. The applications of this love are inexhaustible. The perfect expression of love has yet to be found, except that it has already been expressed by God in Christ. The loving believer is always seeking higher expressions of love for more and more of the peoples of the world. And this quest embraces openness not only to others but to their ideas.

Perhaps the hardest belief-type to love is the believer in no God at all—the atheist. Yet love demands relating and communicating. There is, of course, no way to debate on the existence or nonexistence of God. Neither can "prove" the other wrong; both hold positions based on some form of faith, not on what might be called concrete data. But the thoughtful, self-confident Christian can offer related testimony. The Christian owes it to the atheist to witness to what the awareness of the love of God has done for him or her, and for others. The self-esteeming Christian also owes the atheist a full hearing. Fresh insights may come for both. Love of God and neighbors *and* self creates such a climate.

At the opposite pole from the atheists are the traditionally orthodox believers. On the subject of human depravity, they span a gamut from theologically conservative realists about human nature to hardline believers in total depravity. While meaningful dialogue with the latter may be well nigh impossible, there is much to be gained from the former. Love demands efforts to relate to both. Traditional "conservative" believers have made great contributions to the life of this nation. One thinks of their contribution to the Constitution. It was the conservative's pessimism about human perfection that caused the insistence on the "division of powers." With the "checks and balances" provided between the executive, legislative, and judicial branches of the federal government, none could go too far astray. The Puritan Calvinists among the nation's founders were not naive about human nature, so they set pairs of branches to keep each branch honest. If the President seeks too much power, two other branches of the government rise up with power to make the necessary corrections.

Contemporary Christian belief needs a major movement in the direction of sound self-acceptance, but the realism of the founders of the country still holds. Their spiritual descendants need to hear what this new movement of self-esteem has to say. But they who embrace sound self-esteem need to listen to those who are still skeptical of human nature. The difference between the two groups does not lie in different data about human performance. Rather, it lies in how one interprets the data and states her or his faith.

Sensitive believers in obeying Jesus' command to love others "as thyself " cannot escape a sense of need for the strength and grace needed to love in so lofty a manner. They will honestly confront their potential for evil. They will simply decline to believe that such attraction to temptation is the dominant trait of their inborn character. They will depend on the very image of God within them as a basis for self-esteem. And they will constantly seek the help of God to live up to their divine inheritance.

The traditional view of human nature as depraved has served well in such places as the drafting of the Constitution. But this pessimistic emphasis in contemporary America has wrought havoc in the souls and psyches of untold thousands if not millions. This is especially true with families and supportive religious and social structures crumbling. The doctrine of self-worth bestowed by the Creator is harder and harder for many to believe in depth. The idea of human depravity becomes a final judgment of persons rather than a reason for the seeking of grace. The truth of Jesus' Word about self-love or acceptance is desperately needed, but increasingly difficult to trust. The positive possibilities of persons must be placed alongside the realism of their potential for sin. And this gospel or good news must be shared with all, in love and in powerful witness, regardless of tradition.

It may be argued that the extremes of atheistic humanism and ultrarigid theological conservatism have few adherents in the typical African American community. Doctrinaire rigidity has had no place in the dynamic processes of Black Christian folk belief; the masses have not been attracted to the abstract discourses on either of these extremes. As late as twenty-five years ago, this appraisal of African American folk Christianity may have been true.

But a once powerful cultural momentum favoring faith is dying, while the need for that faith escalates. Traditional patterns of residential segregation are yielding to some degree. And the percentage of Black Americans engaged in higher education is increasing. Doctrinaire adherents to both extremes are making inroads. Megachurches, some with White fundamentalist pastors, thrive on high percentages of Black members. Black atheists and agnostics are not nearly so rare as they once were. Both groups stand in grave jeopardy of profound deficits in self-esteem.

The reasons for this jeopardy are fairly obvious. Atheistic humanists, when faced with personal tragedy, are by choice stripped of the spiritual resources of trust in God's love. The results run the gamut from massive to suicidal depression. Rigid conservative devotees of depravity have been known to turn the focus of this judgment from others to themselves and forget the orthodox remedies. The result, again, has been massive depression or worse. For both groups, this has meant either that life was not worth living or that one was not worthy to continue that life—six of one, half dozen of the other.

The need for deep, "gut" belief in self-worth was already great and growing before the advent of these extremes. Now Black history and Bible-based theology are all the more greatly needed to offset misconceptions and clear away the intellectual obstacles to the saving, healing love of self and neighbor and God. After the history and theology have done their preparatory work, it may be that the Holy Spirit will bless the preaching of the gospel and the loving witness of the church family, to give the hearer holistic faith.

CHAPTER 3

Self-Esteem and Black Caste

Conditions of Birth

"Mother, mother, tell me, am I a nigger?"
"No, my darling, you are not a nigger. . . . You are as good as anybody."[1]

o be born in America with black skin is to be relegated to automatic second-class citizenship. No amount of cultural assimilation can remove the visual reminder to this society that African Americans are not the color white, which is the standard of beauty and the symbol of goodness in the Western world.

Those born into second-class citizenship can respond in several ways. They can be ashamed of their color, and try to compensate for it. They can despair of their color, hate themselves, and engage in self-destructive behaviors. They can rebel against the society at large in antisocial activities like crime, violence, and riotous activity. Or they can conscientiously struggle against the system while affirming themselves.

When this struggle against bigotry is grounded in Christian spirituality, it results in healing and wholeness for the individual and the society. The sermons following in this chapter are intended to remind Black people that though persons in this society are unjustly despised because of the conditions of their birth, they can struggle positively against this reality. For Christians, this struggle is rooted in three spiritual realities: (1) the personal dignity of those created in the image of God; (2) the moral integrity of those who are led by the Holy Spirit and the Word of God; and (3) the spiritual solidarity of Christ himself, who in Luke 4:18-19 identified with the oppressed. With this foundation, African Americans, ethnic minorities, women, and all who are discriminated against because of the conditions of their birth can find wholeness.

Don't Count Me Out

EMIL THOMAS

The number of men who ate was four thousand not counting women and children.
MATTHEW 15:38 (GNB)

When reading Matthew's account of the feeding of the four thousand, I am struck by the editorial comment of the author. When describing the number of persons who dined at this miraculous banquet, the author does not state the total number. He merely mentions that the number of *men* who ate was four thousand. Interestingly, he admits that there was an uncounted number of women and children who never made it into the disciples' tally. For women and children, there was no account or audit. Women and children were not considered or counted. Women and children were neither estimated or evaluated. They were, in essence, counted out.

Everything else was counted! The men were counted; there were four thousand. The bread was counted; there were five loaves. The fish were counted; there were two. The money was counted; an estimate of two hundred denarii was made. Even the leftovers were counted; there were twelve baskets full of fragments. But when it came to the women and children, they didn't make the tally, and were excluded from the totals.

When I was a child growing up in the Black community, there were a number of names that were used to describe one's weight and worth in the community. If you were a flirtatious and romantic male, you were called "fresh." If you were a female with the same tendencies, you were called "fast." If you were considered important, you were called a "Big Negro"; if you were considered unimportant, you were called a "Little Negro" (or something to that effect). But the worst thing that could be said of you was that you were a "no-count Negro." If someone said, "he ain't no count," it meant that you didn't factor into the equation of life. It meant that your person and presence were not important and nonessential. It meant that as an individual you were inconsequential. You didn't matter; you didn't make a difference; you were counted out!

We must come to grips with the reality of being counted out.

How can we respond to this editorial comment of the Gospel writer? How do we interpret this footnote in the holy writ? How do we handle the counted-out crowd?

We must come to grips with the reality *of being counted out.* The author was honest enough to tell us the truth. He gives us the number of men that were fed—four thousand—but then mentions that the women and children were not even included in that number. He may have wanted us to know that in this life, there is a reality to being counted out. In every age, in every society, in every community, there is a caste that is considered to be "no count."

As a matter of fact, what occurred in the text was not at all uncommon. In Bible times, women and children were considered second-class citizens. They did not carry the rights that men carried. They lived in a culture that was dominated by age and gender. The simple fact was that to the people of Jesus' day, women and children just didn't count as much as men.

The Scriptures give ample evidence of this reality. Mark 6:3 gives a tally of Jesus' siblings. It mentions that Jesus had brothers and sisters. It reads, "James, Joseph, Judas, and Simon, *and his sisters.*" Why didn't it give their names or their number? Because they didn't count!

The Gospels also reveal that the disciples sometimes resisted children who wanted to see Jesus. Jesus himself had to speak up and say "Suffer the little children to come unto me and forbid them not, for such is the kingdom of heaven" (Matt. 19:14 AP). But why were they resisted in the first place? Because they didn't count!

Though we live two thousand years later than they, and we consider ourselves progressive, enlightened, and modern, we are not much different than the people of Jesus' day. Our society does not treasure children as we should. We spend more tax dollars for bombs and bullets than we do for bread and books.

We spend more tax dollars for bombs and bullets than we do for bread and books.

Even in some of our churches, the young are made to feel peripheral. How many youths serve on church anniversary committees? How many children participate in worship services or on church programs? How many youths get on pulpit committees? Often when preachers tell their colleagues about the size of their congregation, they are asked the question, "But how many of those are children?" Why is that question asked? Because to some minds, children really don't count. They are an excess number, a surplus figure used only to inflate the number of adults in the congregation—the people who *really* count. A church without children may be large in figures, but they are lacking a future!

Women as well hold a curious role in our current church practice. Women are segregated into Mission Societies, Deaconess Boards, or similar groups. Men can be seen in the highest echelons of leadership, but there is an invisible glass ceiling through which women cannot rise.

It has always puzzled me why women can bake communion bread, fill the communion cups and set the communion table, but they can't serve the communion! It has always struck me as strange that women can sweep around the pulpit, dust off the pulpit, and vacuum behind the pulpit, but they can't preach from the pulpit! Why is that? Because in some areas of service, women have been counted out!

45

Women and children are not the only ones counted out in our society. The poor are counted out. The homeless are counted out. The hungry are counted out. The uneducated and the undereducated are counted out. The so-called "minorities," the Black, Native American, and Asian peoples of the earth, are counted out. "Illegal Aliens" are counted out. "Third-World" people are counted out. Physically challenged people, the so-called "handicapped," are counted out. Seniors are counted out. People with AIDS and HIV are counted out.

As a matter of fact, you can be right in the church and be counted out! Don't get sick for more than two weeks; you might get counted out! Don't make a mistake; you might get counted out! You can even be a member of an auxiliary and be counted out. Here's how you can tell if you've been counted out: if you find out about decisions after they've been made; if everybody gets the news before you; and if when you give your opinion, people begin to look at the ceiling, shuffle paper, and yawn, and then after you speak, they bring the matter to a vote to eliminate your suggestion— you've been counted out!

We should be careful, however, about counting folk out—for the same people we count *out* today, we may need to count *on* tomorrow! Don't neglect anyone today: you may need them tomorrow! Don't disinherit anyone today: you may have to depend on them tomorrow. Don't you count out the women! They are the producers of the race, the nurturers of the nation, and the backbone of humanity! Don't you count out the children! They represent the future of our church, our community, and our culture! Don't count out our senior citizens! They are repositories of experience, storehouses of wisdom, and living examples of God's amazing grace! Those whom you count *out* today, you may have to count *on* tomorrow!

In relation to Black people, America practices a paradoxical politic. The same folk who overlook us in the polls and neglect us in the election are the first ones expecting us to win a gold medal in the Olympics or die on the battlefield of war! America better realize that not only do they need our bodies to work in fields and factories, but they need our brains to build this economy and catapult us into a new postindustrial era of high technology! Men need women; adults need children; White people need Black people; and all of us need Jesus! The counted *out* soon become the counted *on!* We are inextricably bound together—we need one another!

Personally speaking, my ultimate prayer is not that people won't count me out. I've been counted out too many times to even pray that prayer. The reality is that people *will* count you out. People are fickle. People are narrow-minded. People are wishy-washy. People are duplicitous and hypocritical. People are selfish. People are vengeful, unforgiving, mean, and cruel. It is in the very nature of people to count other people out. My prayer is not that people will not count me out, but that Jesus won't count me out!

The good news is that beyond the reality of being counted out, *there is a remedy for being counted out.* Those whom people exclude, Jesus includes! Those whom people write off, Jesus writes in! Those whom people count out, Jesus counts in and counts on!

This truth is tucked into the text of the Gospel story, which later says that *"everyone* ate and had enough" (Matt. 15:37 AP). Even though the women and children were not factored in by these statistically oriented, data-based, information-intensive disciples, Jesus had already made provisions for everyone to be filled and satisfied. The remedy for being counted out is Jesus' counting in!

As a matter of fact, Jesus built his movement with people who came from the culture of the counted out. His disciples were not considered savants of their society. Quite the contrary, the majority of Jesus' followers came from the dispossessed and the disinherited. They were the last, the least, the lowest, the lost, the leftovers, and the locked out. Those closest to him, his twelve disciples, came not from the urban classes, but from the rural masses; not from around Jerusalem, but from around Nazareth; not from Judea, but from Galilee; not from the courts of the Temple, but from the wilderness and the boondocks. When Jesus met them, most of them had dirt under their fingernails, and several of them, no doubt, smelled of fish.

Jesus knew what it was like to be counted out. Jesus himself was from the ranks of the counted out. He was not born in a mansion, but in a manger. He started life not as royalty in Europe, but as a refugee in Africa. The neighborhood where he grew up was so remote and backward that folk wondered out loud, "Can anything good come out of Nazareth?" Though he made the world he never owned a home, for he said "The foxes have holes, and the birds of the air have nests, but the son of man hath nowhere to lay his head." Jesus was a card-carrying member of the caste of the counted out.

Perhaps that is why the authorship of this book is attributed to Matthew. He of all the Gospel writers would not miss this point! Matthew himself was from the community of the counted out. Matthew was a tax collector and a publican. He was considered by his fellow Jews as a collaborator with the occupying Roman imperialists, the equivalent of the biggest "Uncle Tom" of his day. But one day, a miracle occurred. Jesus passed by while Matthew was sitting at his table collecting taxes. People had excluded him, but Jesus included him! People had written him off, but Jesus wrote him in! His people had counted him out, but Jesus counted him in! Jesus simply said, "Follow me," and Matthew "left all, rose up, and followed him" (Matt. 9:9 AP).

Maybe that's why this book was written to Jewish Christians. Maybe Matthew was saying to them, "Remember, you were once counted out! Now just because there are a lot of Gentiles coming into the church, don't count them out!"

It is possible to think of the miracles of Jesus as redemptive remedies for the counted out; for in every one of his miracles, he includes the excluded, writes in the written off, and counts in the counted out!

The woman with the issue of blood had been counted out. The doctors had counted her out. Her community had counted her out. For twelve long years, she lived the life of the counted out. But when she touched the hem of his garment, she was healed and counted back in. Jesus said, "Daughter, your faith has made you whole, go in peace" (AP).

The man at the pool of Bethesda had been counted out. For thirty-eight years he lived among the counted out at the pool. Not only was he counted out by society, but he had even counted himself out, for when Jesus asked, "Would you be made whole?" he had no direct answer, only a pitiful litany of alibis. But Jesus stopped by the pool and said: "I'll count you back in, but first you must take some initiative yourself. Take up your bed and walk."

Lazarus had certainly been counted out. They counted four days since he had died. They even said that the stench of impossibility hovered around his grave. Jesus showed up after the funeral, only to be told off by Martha in the middle of the road. "If you had been here, my brother would never have died." But Jesus just stood there and said, "You're going too far, now Martha, for not only have you counted Lazarus out, now you are counting me out. You don't know who I am! I am the resurrection and the life. If any one believeth in me, though he were dead, yet shall he live." When he called Lazarus' name, he was miraculously raised to life. Jesus had counted him back in!

Perhaps someone is now thinking: "All of that sounds good, preacher. We know that Jesus can give spiritual encouragement to us when we are rejected by the world. But on a historical basis, will it always be like this? Will we always have to deal with the sociological reality of being counted out? Will we always have to appeal to heavenly help for spiritual remedies when we are counted out? Will the counted out ever totally transcend their circumstances and situations?"

I believe that one day, there will be a rally for the counted out.

Yes, I believe so. *I believe that one day, there will be a rally for the counted out.* I believe that one day this world shall be changed. I believe that human history will be revolutionized and redeemed. I believe that human systems and societies will one day be saved. I believe that one day there will be a rally for the counted out at the end of time. The book of Revelation is a program for that rally!

Though I've had to fight for my rights in this society and on this earth, I don't believe in "Bogarting" my way into God's program. I want to be invited and included on God's program. So I did some research. I had to look in the book because I wanted to see if I was on the program. I had to find a place where I could personally participate in the program. I had to find a group in which I could perfectly fit in. I'll give you the results of my research. I'll show you where I'm on the program.

As I read the book of Revelation, I saw seven churches and seven angels, but I'm not in that number. I saw four and twenty elders, but I'm not in that number. I saw one hundred and forty-four thousand, but I'm not in that number. Jehovah's Witnesses erroneously assert that some of them are in that number, but that number is made up of ethnic Jews. There are twelve thousand from the tribe of Judah; twelve thousand from Reuben; twelve thousand from Gad; twelve thousand from Asher; twelve thousand from Naphtali; twelve thousand from Manasseh; twelve thousand from Simeon; twelve thousand from Levi; twelve thousand from Issachar; twelve thousand from Zebulun; twelve thousand from Joseph; and twelve thousand from Benjamin—but I'm not in that number.

But wait a minute! There is another number. It is an un-counted number. It is a number greater than any person can number. That number is from every nation, tribe, people, and language. That number stands before the throne of the lamb. That number will never hunger or thirst again. That number will never feel the scorching heat of the sun again. And for that number, God will wipe away all tears from their eyes.

Like the apostle John, I asked, "What is this number?" I heard an angel say, "These are they that have come up through great tribulation, and have washed their robes in the blood of the Lamb."

I said to myself, "That's my part on the program! That's the kind of crowd where I can fit in perfectly! I'm going to be in that number, when the saints go marching in!"

On Starting from the Bottom, Or Bethlehem Revisited

HENRY H. MITCHELL

And she brought forth her firstborn son, and wrapped him in swaddling clothes, and laid him in a manger; because there was no room for them in the inn.

LUKE 2:7

Since this isn't Christmas, and we're not bound by seasonal traditions, let me invite you to go with me to Bethlehem, this time with a whole new set of attitudinal rules. Let's have no sentimentality. No carols with "the poor baby wakes," and no spirituals with "Oh, po' lil' Jesus." And yes, no getting angry at the desk clerk at the Bethlehem Inn. Let's start from zero and, with no Christmas biases, look at it like it is, as we say.

In the first place, no small "home town" hotel will ever be big enough to hold all the folk who left that town and settled in the big city. And most certainly it would never hold them all at once. So it's only logical to follow a policy of "No reservations, no motel room." The desk clerks are only doing their job. There's nothing at all personal about this rejection. (Now, of course, if the *right* customers show up without a reservation, managers have been known to *make* a room, but not for a one-time customer, and hardly for a pregnant peasant.) To *ask* this clerk for a room under the present circumstances is to act like you can order up miracles on demand. We all know better.

You are no doubt saying to yourself, this can't possibly be the beginning of a serious sermon; there has to be some *good* news in this *some*where. And you're right; there is some good news, like the manger, for instance. It's a feed box, but a cradle is just as much a box as a manger, only with rockers. And the mattress is fresh hay, which is clean and sweet. When I was a little boy, I used to walk through the fields and *eat* the soft ends of hay stalks. They were good to the taste and nourishing besides. Let's not worry about the manger. It's a plus.

51

And let's not worry about the rest of it. Take the swaddling cloths for instance—the diapers. So far as I know, a diaper was and is only a diaper. Of course, they have started making these wasteful plastic disposables. But even now there are no high fashion "Brooks Brothers" versions of an infant's underthings. All babies get dirty and get changed the same way. There is absolutely no reason whatever to suggest that the baby Jesus was any different.

The same can be said for the menu; a healthy mother's milk is a healthy mother's milk. Period. The "kitchens" that God made for feeding babies are all the same. In fact, the Lord has fixed it so that even mothers who are nearing starvation can find a little something to give their nursing infants. The miracle of mammary nourishment is spread across all nations and races and classes of mothers. So Jesus had the best of food and enough of it.

On this trip to Bethlehem, we find no reason for pity, for Baby Jesus has two loving parents (the most any child can have), the usual ten fingers and ten toes, and the normal feelings and mental equipment. In a word, let's not pity our Savior or ourselves, even though a great many of us started at the socioeconomic bottom. Given what Jesus had, so far as raising children is concerned, it could even be a parental advantage to start at the same kind of lowest point on the totem pole of human society.

Given what Jesus had, so far as raising children is concerned, it could even be a parental advantage to start at the same kind of lowest point on the totem pole of human society.

To tell the truth, I believe that God *meant* for Jesus to start at the bottom of society. In addition to what I have already mentioned, there were some distinct advantages: God wanted to identify with the oppressed through a human Son. Existential philosophers would easily explain this on the basis that people at the bottom always see a society more accurately than others. They have no vested interests to maintain, and no positions of privilege to protect. Jesus' matchless clarity of insight about people and society was at least partially due to his being a "manger kid," accurately sizing his world up, as first seen from the very bottom.

One sees this advantage in some of the slave narratives, the memoirs of escaped slaves. They had amazing understanding of how owning slaves actually rotted character. Ex-slaves such as Austin Steward analyzed how slaves made an owner's children lazy and self-indulgent; how it tempted husbands to debauchery, drinking, and gambling, while squandering great fortunes and bringing families down in disgrace. Steward described how the sin of owning slaves even haunted sensitive souls on their deathbeds. His slave's-eye view from the bottom up was psychiatrically and ethically far more accurate than that of the historians of his day, or that of novelists like the author of *Gone with the Wind*. Jesus' astounding wisdom came from the same position in society as that of our slave foreparents.

Jesus' start at the bottom even fits best with God's goal of the salvation of the world. If Jesus had been king, he would not have been accessible to the masses. Even a middle-class merchant's family would still have left him out of the reach of many. But all may feel close to him, regardless of the condition of their birth, because Jesus started at a level where all could feel free to approach him, with no fear of being put down.

One is forced to wonder just how much Matthew understood this. He certainly provided often overlooked data for the belief that God very specifically meant for Jesus to be identified with the bottom. In the genealogy he provides in his Gospel, Matthew breaks with normal tradition and mentions four *women* in the first six verses! That's different! And *these* women are not even respectable by some societies' standards. For instance, take Rahab; she was at one time an outright prostitute. Then there are people like Ruth and Tamar, and Bathsheba, the unprotesting widow of the murdered Uriah. All of these women have what might be called character flaws, and they are in Jesus' family. Indeed, almost everyone in Jesus' family tree had flaws. Matthew is telling us of a racial mixture and strange arrangements in the ancestry of a Savior whose background was as mixed and as questionable as ours. I believe our Maker had that in the plan also.

Jesus carried his identification with the folks at the bottom even further. In the parable of the last judgment, Jesus said the unforgettable words, "Inasmuch as ye did it unto the least of my loved ones, ye did it unto *me!*" (Matt. 25:40 AP). Privileged people need to be careful how they treat the oppressed; they may be messin' with Jesus when they do that.

I call to remembrance two teenage boys who picked cotton and cut grapes in the fields near the church where I served in Fresno, California. When they came home all dusty and dirty, they bore no resemblance to the leaders they were to become. But now one is a nationally renowned computer specialist; the other is an influential psychiatrist. Looking at Bethlehem, one is reminded that you can never tell *how* high a "manger kid" will go in life. We would do well to treat the very lowest in our world with kindness and compassion; we could be mistreating our Savior.

This also suggests that the All-Wise God, who is no respecter of persons, plans to restock the leadership genius of the world from *all* of its classes and races. Nobody can have so much money that her or his children can be guaranteed to be geniuses. And you never know when some manger kid's achievements will surpass most, if not all, of the children of the powerful. The Creator alone passes out the genius, and gives it to whomsoever fits the Divine Plan.

Never mind where you *started;* just try to figure out where God wants you to end up. One of the very greatest preachers of the twentieth century, Gardner C. Taylor, tells of seeing an old friend in an audience where he preached. When the service closed, they ran to each other and embraced. Dr. Taylor and his friend were in tears. When last they had met, this friend was still struggling financially to stay in school. The friend's parents were illiterate, and he grew up quite literally beside a cotton patch. Time after time he had narrowly escaped having to leave school because of no funds.

Now he was the chief of surgery at a famous medical school. These were tears of joy over the way God had blessed both of them beyond their wildest imaginations. They knew their great blessings came from God, and mangers and cotton patch cabins are no obstacle to God's amazing, gracious distribution of intellectual gifts.

I suppose the most important reason for this revisitation of Bethlehem and the stable is to help us celebrate our own mangers and stables—our own obscure and unimpressive beginnings. You see, if we can be glad about our own starting places, we need never be ashamed before anybody. If we can rejoice over our own little tiny birthplaces, we can be glad God made *us* there, and we can be willing to go back if ever the need should arise. This makes us invulnerable, and unafraid of the changes forced on us in an oppressive society.

You see, if we can be glad about our own starting places, we need never be ashamed before anybody. If we can rejoice over our own little tiny birthplaces, we can be glad God made *us* there, and we can be willing to go back if ever the need should arise.

We can be free of the fear that we might have to go back where we started. But we can be like the rabbit in that old tale told by our ancestors. When the powerful, vicious fox was about to have his lunch on fresh rabbit, the rabbit pleaded: "Oh please, Mr. Fox, do anything to me but that." This appealed to the cruel instincts of the fox. He could just see the rabbit suffering from the thorns of the briar patch. The fox could imagine Mr. Rabbit's terrible misery, so he threw him into the thicket. It was a great victory for Brer Rabbit, because he was born and reared in briars. He knew how to deal with briars, and he laughed at the fox as he ran and leaped to safety.

You know, I like to think I'm a manger kid too. And if the preaching and teaching get rough, or somebody tries to make me sell my soul in a compromise, I can still go back to my Bethlehem or my briar patch. I can still cut a rafter or set a door. I can still drive a truck or mop a floor. I *have* done it, and I wouldn't be too proud or heartbroken to do it again. All manger kids who are thankful to God for their mangers, can survive any time, anywhere, and under any circumstances.

Some years ago I had a visit with my two young Fresno friends in North Jersey, where they had both relocated after college and graduate school. They were doing exceedingly well. The home of the computer specialist where we were visiting was located by a lake. Their little boy could go fishing while his parents watched through the kitchen window.

I rather expected that they would regale me with tales of their great accomplishments. To my surprise, they spent the entire evening talking about raisin vineyards and cotton patches. They literally *celebrated* the life out of which they had come. They were glad about their Bethlehem. Downsized corporations could terminate their jobs, but they were so firmly planted on their beginnings that they *knew* God would care for them some way, somehow. Meanwhile they were glad to be God's children, even if it meant going back to one of their many manual skills.

Speaking of Jesus' willingness to step down, the apostle Paul wrote what may have become a great hymn of the early church. He said, "Let this mind be in you, which was also in Christ Jesus: Who, being in the form of God, did not consider equality with God, a status to be clung to."

Rather, he joined the people at the bottom, and assumed the role of a lowly servant, and was made in the likeness of a human being.

And being in human form, he humbled himself, and became obedient to death itself, even the death of the cross. Wherefore God has highly exalted him, and given him a name which is above every name: That at the name of Jesus every knee should bow, of things in heaven, and things in earth, and things under the earth; And that every tongue should confess that Jesus Christ is Lord, to the glory of God the Father. (Phil. 2:8-11 AP)

Thank you, Lord, for taking the embarrassment out of Bethlehem beginnings and manger cradles.

We thank you, Lord, for the renewal of our self-image.

We praise you, Lord, for a Savior who has borne our griefs and carried our sorrows.

We thank you, Lord, for a life filled with surprises that have lifted us out of the mire of poverty.

Bless your name, Lord, for permission and power to go all the way to excellence.

We bless your Holy name, Lord, no matter where we start or what kind of family tree we have, you held us in the palm of your hands.

Glory be! Lord, for a way out of no way.

Glory be! Lord, for the joy of knowing that it does not yet appear what we or our children shall yet be.

Glory be to God for Jesus' rise from the bottom to be King of Kings and Lord of Lords.

Hallelujah! Hallelujah! Amen!

Questions for Discussion

Don't Count Me Out

1. The sermon lists a number of groups that are counted out. Are you a member of any of these groups? Which one(s)? Have you ever been counted out? State one experience in which you were counted out because of the conditions of your birth.

2. Are there any other reasons why people are counted out that were not mentioned in the sermon? If so, what are they?

3. Have you ever counted people out because of something over which they had no control? Recount the experience. Why did you count them out? What happened to those who were counted out? How has that affected you since that time?

4. The sermon states that since Jesus made provisions for the counted out in his miracle, they were counted in. What have you done to include the excluded?

On Starting from the Bottom, Or Bethlehem Revisited

1. What are the disadvantages of starting from the bottom? What are the advantages?
2. Where were you born? What city? In a hospital? In a home? How do you feel about where you were born? Are you proud? Are you ashamed? Why?
3. Did you know that Jesus had a prostitute named Rahab in his family tree? How do you think that affected Jesus? Are there any "shady characters" in your family tree? Are there any "outcasts" in your family? How does your family deal with them? How does this affect your concept of your family? Of yourself?
4. When was the last time you visited the place where you were born? How did you feel? Were you embarrassed? Proud? Emotional? Have you ever thanked God for where and how you were born?
5. State three reasons to give God thanks for the conditions of your birth.

CHAPTER 4

Self-Esteem and Black Characteristics

Loving the Way We Look

We do not believe that there is any hope for any race of people who do not believe they look like God.[1]

The words of the nineteenth century A.M.E. Bishop, Henry McNeil Turner, reveal that we are not the first to believe that there is a correlation between a people's evaluation of their looks and their self-esteem. To reject one's own physical features is to reject both one's self and the handiwork of God. This chapter contains sermons that affirm that the descendants of Africans and others can love the way they look, because it is appropriate to respond to God's *creation* with *appreciation* and *celebration*.

Acts 17:26 states that the *creation* was the result not of a cosmic accident but of a divine design: "And [God] hath made of one blood all nations of men for to dwell on all the face of the earth, and hath determined the times before appointed, and the bounds of their habitation." Genesis 1:31 states that God's own attitude toward creation was *appreciation*: "And God saw every thing that he had made, and, behold, it was very good." Psalm 139:14 is traditionally accepted as David's own *celebration* of the very way he was made: "I will praise thee; for I am fearfully and wonderfully made."

Appreciation of God's creation is not only a religious impulse; it is a rational imperative! A simple self-esteem syllogism reveals the soundness of the logic behind loving one's looks:

Premise 1:   God designed the physical features of every ethnic group.

Premise 2:   All of God's designs are essentially good.

Conclusion: The physical features of every ethnic group are essentially good.

The Skin I'm In

EMIL THOMAS

Can the Ethiopian change his skin, or the leopard his spots?
JEREMIAH 13:23

Hello. Allow me to introduce myself. My name is Lumumba and I'm a leopard. I dropped by to share my testimony with you today. Due to centuries of information that has negatively affected your psyche, I decided it was time that we had a conversation.

I know that it is rather unusual for an animal to appear in the order of worship. I'm sure that it seems strange for a cat to come to church. But I believe that there is a crisis, and I've been commissioned by God to get a message through to you today. You see, it is possible that your mental static can cause you to miss the heavenly frequency. It is possible for people to become so ingrained with inaccuracies that they are oblivious to the obvious. It is possible for people to have eyes and not be able to see, ears but not be able to hear. Whenever this happens, there is a crisis of communication, and then God will use any means necessary to get people's attention.

When Moses was feeding his flock on the backside of the Midianite desert, there was a crisis of communication. God had to electrify a bush and use it as a public address system to get Moses' attention. When Belshazzar ruled Babylon, there was a crisis of communication. God sent a hand to write on the wall and the prophet Daniel to interpret to Belshazzar that he had been weighed in the balances and found wanting. At Jesus' baptism there was a crisis of communication about who Jesus was, so God had to open up the heavens, send the Spirit in the form of a dove and declare from on high, "This is my beloved Son, in whom I am well pleased." When there is a crisis of communication, God will use any means necessary to get humanity's attention.

So don't be offended today that a leopard has come to church to deliver a message to the people of God. After all, you are a people of faith, so you know that with God all things are possible. If God used a donkey to bring Balaam to greater comprehension, if God used a rooster to bring Peter to greater conviction, surely God can use a leopard to bring Ethiopians to a greater consciousness of their self-worth! Turn on your sanctified imagination and listen to the testimony of a leopard. Your tribe has a rich repertoire of names. Some have called themselves Negroes; others, Black; others, People of Color; and others, African Americans. But for continuity with the biblical record, I will call you all Ethiopians. After all, in antiquity, all of Africa was once known as Ethiopia.

Now, even though I am a leopard and you are Ethiopians, we do have some things in common. Both of us are packaged in unique skin. The skin I'm in is spotted. The skin you're in is dark. Because I'm packaged in spotted skin and you are packaged in a variety of darker skin shades, people react to us in extreme ways. On one hand, we may be envied; on the other hand, we may be exterminated. On one hand, we may liked; on the other hand, we may be lynched. On one hand, we may be mimicked; on the other hand, we may be murdered. For some reason, people have extreme reactions to the skin we're in.

But we are not only linked together by the skin we're in, we are also locked together by the scripture we're in. God used us as portraits of immutability and unchangeability. We were united in this Bible passage to be paradigms of strength and steadfastness. In Jeremiah 13:23, God asked the question, "Can the Ethiopian change his skin, or the leopard his spots?" The answer that God sought was a resounding *NO!* It was then and is now unconscionable and unnecessary for Ethiopians to change their skin or leopards to change their spots. Yet God posed that question over five hundred years before Christ, and we need to believe that God wants to hear the same answer even today.

That's the reason that I am here today. I think that some of you are trying to get out of your skin. Some of you are trying to modify your package of skin to the point that you will be unrecognizable as children of Africa. Some of you are trying to bleach yourself blackless! Some of you are using cosmetics to camouflage your characteristics! Some of you are seeking to dermatologically deny your Ethiopian distinctiveness! Some of you are erasing your Ethiopian insignia. Some of you are trying to get out of the skin you're in!

Well I don't want to be in this scripture by myself. It is one scripture in which I had a positive affiliation with humanity and now you are getting ready to leave me in it alone. I came to call you back to Jeremiah 13:23. I came to call you back into your package of skin and this passage of scripture. Moreover, I came to call you back to who you are and whose you are. I came to tell you that you can have peace, happiness, and joy in the skin that you're in.

The only way that I know to do this is through my testimony. I want you to know that God has kept me and blessed me in the skin that I'm in. Now I know that I am not as smart as you. I do not possess your intelligence. I do not possess your ingenuity. I do not possess your insights in philosophy, science, or technology. I know that you were created a little lower than the angels. I know that you are humans and that I am an animal. I know that God created you to have dominion over creation as heaven's faithful steward of the temporal world. But don't get so lifted up and lofty that you forget your mortality. You are part spirit but you are also part flesh. I may not have the ability to do plastic surgery or the technology to change my spots, but I do have enough sense to know that God made me with spots, and God don't make no junk! So please give me some credit, and listen to the testimony of this lowly leopard.

My testimony is that I am not worried about the skin that I am in because God has blessed me and God has kept me! Maybe, just maybe, if you see why I stay in the skin that I'm in, you will be happy in the skin that you're in, and we can both stay together in Jeremiah 13:23.

I stay in the skin that I'm in because it's *beautiful!*

If the skin I'm in were repulsive and repugnant, unsightly and ugly, unappealing and unattractive, I just might be ashamed of it. If I wasn't so beautiful, I might ask God for the capacity of the chameleon to shift my shade according to my setting and scenery. If I wasn't so beautiful, I might ask God to give me the instinct to hide my head in the sand, as ostriches were once rumored to do. If I wasn't so beautiful, I might ask God to give me the urge of the hermit crab to go crawl up into a shell somewhere. But a leopard's skin is not homely, it's handsome. I'm not gruesome, I'm gorgeous. I'm not loathsome, I'm lovely; I'm not foul, I'm fine. I stay in the skin that I'm in because it's beautiful.

If some say my skin isn't beautiful, then why do so many humans want to wear it? People are hunting me and the members of my species because they want to turn us into leopard-skin coats, leopard-skin hats, leopard-skin dresses, suits, purses, and shoes. If people want to kill me just so that they can get into the skin I'm in, I must be beautiful indeed!

Have you ever taken a close look at a leopard skin? It's an amazing thing to behold. We have skin that can have a variety of background colors, producing a coat of hair that can range from a deep bronze to a bright gold. On this backdrop are speckled and spotted rosettes of shimmering black markings that are patterned differently on each leopard. Sometimes when I just go down to a pond, it isn't just to get a drink of water, but to catch a glimpse of my fine reflection in the pool. Let the tiger have her stripes. Let the lion have his silky mane. To my mind neither of them is more splendid or magnificent than me and my spots!

Now before you call me conceited or accuse me of arrogance, have you looked in your mirror lately? I've got to give it to you, you

Ethiopians are also a sight to behold. If your skin weren't so beautiful, then why are so many people spending so much time and money to have darker skin? Why are persons making millions of dollars selling suntan lotion, creating tanning parlors, and advertising Caribbean vacations where people can get a deep, dark tan while they have fun in the sun? Somebody must think you're beautiful if they want their skin to be similar to your skin.

Just take a look at the countless tones and undertones in the sky of modern-day Ethiopians! You have skin that ranges across the entire spectrum of skin color, from ebony black to mahogany brown; from polished bronze to golden brown; from café au lait to mellow yellow; from light and bright to darned near white. You who call yourselves African Americans are beautiful in all the shades that God made you. Your skin may be light like Kimberly Aiken or Angela Davis. Your skin may be brown like Coretta Scott King or Nelson Mandela. Your skin may be black like Wesley Snipes or Marcus Garvey. Your skin may even be bronze, which is the color that John ascribed to Jesus when he saw him in his vision in Revelation 1:15. But whatever the shade or tone, the skin you're in is beautiful!

No one has created a work of art more beautiful than anything that God has made! Whenever you look in the mirror, you ought to praise God, because you are looking at God's handiwork. Rance Allen, powerful Pentecostal preacher, pastor, and musician, says it this way:

> "I looked in the mirror, and what did I see?
> Another one of God's miracles looking back at me!"[2]

I stay in the skin I'm in because it's *practical*.

You see, the spotted pattern on a leopard's skin is not for the sake of raw aesthetics or pure vanity, though it is indeed beautiful to behold. The skin I'm in has a practical purpose. The skin I'm in helps me to survive on planet earth. You see, leopards like me live in the savannas and grasslands of Africa. We live in the jungles and thickets of Asia. I even have a cousin called the Jaguar that lives in the tropical forests of Central and South America. The skin I'm in is an essential tool whether I'm hunting or hiding. So I believe I'll stay in it! The tigers have stripes, but they are an endangered species. The lions have manes but they too are threatened by extinction. But we leopards are still plentiful in our natural habitats. These old leopard spots keep me hunting and hiding, surviving and thriving. I think I'll just keep them—they're practical, and as you well know, it's a jungle out there.

Now, my Ethiopian friends, your skin is just as practical. But a lot of you don't know that! You have been victimized by a racist system that tells you that everything dark or black is bad, so you think that applies to your skin as well. This racism has become so powerful that it has made it difficult for God to communicate to you that you are marvelously and wonderfully made.

Western culture has placed a negative evaluation on the color black. The black cat is bad luck. A black comedy is gruesome, vile, and wicked. The bad guys wear black hats and ride black horses. To cheat or double-cross some folk is to blackmail them. To arbitrarily exclude people from a group is to blackball them. The black list is for revenge and rejection. Black magic is Satanic and demonic. The black market is the illegal economy. The black sheep is the ne'er-do-well of the family, and a black mark is a tainted or tarnished record.

This type of negative defining can blind you to the fact that the skin you're in is not bad because it is darker than others. On the contrary, your skin is full of practical benefits. All skin, hair, and eye color comes from a substance known as melanin. Melanin is brown in color, and the less you have, the less pigmentation you have in your skin. The skin is the largest organ in the body. A one-hundred-and-fifty-pound adult male has about twenty square feet of skin. Melanin is important because it protects the skin from the dangerous and damaging ultraviolet rays of the sun. At the same time, it permits longer exposure to the health-giving rays of the sun, and melanin allows humans to assimilate vitamin D through the skin. The melanin-filled skin you're in is not a burden, it's a blessing. It's not a problem, it's practical.

I believe I'll keep the skin I'm in because, beyond being beautiful and practical, it is also *natural!*

This is the way God made me! These spots are in the chemistry of my chromosomes. It is my very nature to have spots. My spots are not defective, they are a part of the original design of my species. So why should I change my spots? They are a natural inheritance that contributes to my unique identity in the created order.

My Ethiopian friends, the skin that you are in is also natural. Why change it? If your skin is naturally dark, why try to lighten it, brighten it, and whiten it? If your eyes are naturally dark, why change them through the cosmetic application of lightly colored contact lenses? If the eyes are the windows to the soul, how can others see clearly into the sanctuary of your spirit through stained-glass windows? If your fleecy locks of hair are naturally dark, why change their natural beauty with unnatural treatments? If you are going to use cosmetics, why not use them to *enhance* your natural beauty rather than *escape* it? Wear your deeply colored skin and enhance its tones and undertones! Wear your beautifully colored eyes as clear and unclouded lenses to the life that is within you! Wear your fleecy locks of hair! Show their strength through some plaits, braids, designs, and patterns that fit the texture of the hair God gave you! Forget about plastic surgery to diminish your nose, cut down your lips or reduce the fullness and prominence of features that identify you as an Ethiopian. Be yourself, love yourself, and present yourself as an example of the handiwork of God who made you!

In conclusion, I must remind you that this skin problem is not an animal problem: it is uniquely a human problem. With humans there is this strange obsession with skin. Some reject humans in different skin colors. Others of you even reject the skin that you are in. That's because what had been labeled a skin problem is not really a skin problem at all. The problem is not the skin, but within the person who is in the skin! The problem is sin. You see, when sin is within, people will have problems with skin. But according to Samuel, "Man looketh on the outward appearance, but the LORD looketh on the heart" (I Sam. 16:7).

God has not spent a lot of time throughout history dealing with skin. However, God has spent a lot of time trying to root out the sin that is beneath the skin. Finally, God's ultimate decision was to put a Son into skin to move us beyond sin. "The Word was made flesh, and dwelt among us" (John 1:14). So *in skin* Jesus was born in Bethlehem. *In skin* he spent his infancy in Africa. *In skin* he was baptized by John in the Jordan. *In skin* he changed a woman of Samaria into an ambassador of the Kingdom. But with all of this, sin still reigned within the skin of humanity. So one Friday, he took an old rugged cross and marched up a hill called Calvary. An African saw Jesus falter under the weight of the cross and was compelled to share the burden. They spat on Jesus' skin. They nailed his skin. They tore open his skin with a spear, and the blood came streaming down. And there, on the cross, Jesus took on himself the sins of humanity, and died for every one of you! That skin was taken off the cross. That skin was laid in Joseph's new tomb. That skin was still all night Friday, all day Saturday, and all night Saturday night. But early on Sunday morning, *in skin*, he rose from the grave with all power in his hands! So much power that if you're Black, you don't have to get back! So much power that if you're brown, you can stay around! So much power that you can be white (or any other color) and all right! You can stay in whatever skin you're in! Sin's dominion has been defeated! Sin's debt has been paid!

God's Handiwork: Me!

HENRY H. MITCHELL

I will praise thee; for I am fearfully and wonderfully made: marvellous are thy works; and that my soul knoweth right well.

PSALM 139:14

Twenty-five years ago, we had a great civil rights revolution, and one of the most positive cries heard was, "Black is beautiful." People who had once been ashamed of their African features stopped frying their hair and bleaching their skin. It seemed a powerful, healing movement, but it's over already. People are back where they started; the only difference is that the price of a Jherri curl or a wave is astronomical compared to what a "gas job" used to cost. The question now is, What caused the failure of the movement toward wholehearted acceptance of our African features?

One answer, and perhaps the most important, is that this was a fad, with roots in political and social slogans. There were no changeless principles at stake, so we drifted back to where our deepest feelings had been all the while. We had never really changed. It never had occurred to most of us that there were changeless religious principles involved here—that it matters in eternity how we accept the handiwork of God, who made us.

To say we don't like the way we were made, and that we wish we looked like some other race, is heresy—a blasphemous way to look at the part of Creation called Me! God said everything made was good (Gen. 1:31). If way down deep we hate the way God made us, we hate the One who made us just as deeply, no matter how much we say we love the Lord.

Now we understand that everybody wants to be attractive; no sane soul on earth actually wants to be ugly. But what is ugly? Every group of people has its own set of definitions, and we need to have ours. If we keep on hating ourselves as we are, we'll wind up finding that we haven't loved anybody else, including our neighbors and our God. So let's look at a solid, biblical basis for loving God, as well as seeing ourselves for the beautiful people we are.

One of the psalmists, possibly David, engages in meditation, in the midst of which he cries out, "I will praise you, because I am awesomely and wonderfully made. Marvelous are your works, as shown in creatures like me, and that my soul knows right well!" (Ps. 139:14 AP). No true believer can ever look at any of God's creation without awe and wonder. A moving hymn says it very well:

> Then sings my soul, my Savior God to thee,
> How great thou art, How great thou art!

Just as "The heavens declare the glory of God, and the skies display God's handiwork" (Ps. 19:1 AP), so also does the face of *every* God-crafted human being. Each has a beauty and dignity all its own. When we look in the mirror, it's time once again to sing praise to our Creator in these same words, "How great thou art!"

All of us are born pretty, and I challenge you especially to show me a Black baby who isn't downright handsome. This is a work of God!

One easily recognizes God's handiwork in special examples. I dare to declare that there are no ugly babies. *All* of us are born pretty, and I challenge you especially to show me a Black baby who isn't downright handsome. This is a work of God!

The same is true with a bride in her bridal gown, or a brother in uniform. We have no trouble seeing the beauty of *every* bride. Yet they are the same people in street clothing. Why is it that suddenly we see them as less than beautiful, once they take off the gown?

The psalmist was right! We are all awesomely and wonderfully constructed. The Creator was altogether accurate when appraising all that was created by saying, "That's good." And to deny this not only shuts us off from God; it is horribly cruel to ourselves and to other people.

I cringe every time I hear a parent screaming at a child about "greasing those ashy arms." *All* human beings have the same skin scales or flakes; it's just that some show up more than others. One can advise a child on good grooming without putting the child down by the very tone of one's voice.

It is cruel to fuss at a child about what we heartlessly refer to as "kinky or nappy hair," or "liver lips." To ridicule *any* feature made by God hurts far more deeply than we have any notion.

I think of the "bowl" haircut my wonderful father administered to me when I was in the second grade. I got no help from eyes that squinted and seemed to slant, because we didn't know I needed glasses. To my African American schoolmates I strongly resembled a Chinese. They trooped down the street pointing fingers at me and crying, "Ching chung Chinieman, eats dead rats. Chews them up like ginger snaps." The memory still scars my soul these sixty-seven years later.

Perhaps these children didn't know any better, but every mature adult should carefully teach them not to hurl insults against both the Maker and the made, the other children. It is even worse to hate one's *own* physical features, and yet parents and others teach children to do it every day. Such had been the case with an eleven-year-old boy who came to a revival one night and heard my word about full, or Negroid, lips. I'm very happy with my full mouth, and I make no bones about the fact that the same thick skin that makes full mouths also wrinkles much less than others. I shared the ghetto wisdom that "Black don't crack." The full mouths of Black folks also give one more to kiss than thin lips. In recent years this fact has moved many non-Africans to seek injections to make their mouths fuller than they were naturally. Our eleven-year-old listened intently and was deeply impressed.

A few days later, his father reported that after the church service his son came through the door at home shouting, "Look! The most kissable lips in the world!" Then the father recalled how this same boy had seemed so pensive and engaged in deep thought at an early age. He had walked around with his lips pursed much of the time. It was now obvious that someone had taught him not to be ashamed of his lips. This father thanked God that a word from the psalmist had freed his boy of the awful curse of self-hatred over how he was made. He never puckered or pursed his lips again.

One of the most wonderful things about the street culture of many in the Black ghetto was—in days gone by—the rule about respecting every human being, just as she or he is. It went back to our African ancestors' rules about bringing children up to respect and stay on pleasant terms with *every* human spirit. One greets *every*body one passes, and one never makes fun of anybody.

In my boyhood ghetto, there was a woman with a huge growth hanging from the side of her face and head, all the way almost to her shoulder. She covered it with a cloth, but one could still see the hideous contrast between a side with a lovely face and a side where the weight of the growth pulled eyes and mouth into gruesome contortions. I am proud to say that this ghetto rule of respect prevailed. I never ever saw anyone of any age making fun of this woman. If they had, they would have been roundly scolded for disrespect of one created in God's image.

To show disrespect for or make fun of a human is not just bad manners. It is blasphemy. And it has destructive influence on the person ridiculing, as well as the person ridiculed. No one deserves to be disrespected on the basis of physical characteristics for which she or he has no actual responsibility in the first place.

The good news and antidote for this bad habit is to keep foremost in one's mind the psalmist's powerful affirmation: we *are* awesomely and wonderfully made, and that includes all the physical features we have: facial features, color, hair, skin, and anything else you want to mention. Just to look in the mirror and ponder the creation of the teeth we brush or the eyes we see with is cause to burst forth in praise: "Marvellous are thy works; and that my soul knoweth right well!" (Ps. 139:14*b*).

That includes our complexions; "Black is beautiful" is far more than a Black nationalist slogan. Black *is* beautiful, as we have already noted, along with Solomon in the Songs 1:5. And the world's population is mostly deeply colored, and always was. The first human beings were close to what we call Black, which was certainly true of the original Canaanites also.

In Jericho one day I asked my tour director, Wyatt T. Walker, what those "Africans" were doing there. He replied, "*What* Africans?" He rightly assumed that every African American should know that the Midianites and Moabites and many other ancient Canaanites were Black. Doesn't the book of Numbers (12:1) tell us that Moses' Midianite wife was an Ethiopian, dark by definition?

And doesn't the book of Revelation portray our Lord as a person of color (1:15)? In this vision his feet were like burnished brass. How else could he be, with all that Canaanite ancestry mentioned in the first chapter of Matthew? And the Hebrews were brown to start with. Sallman's very popular paintings of the head of Christ are far whiter than anybody of Jesus' day. Black children need to know this to build pride in their own color.

The same can be said of their hair. Revelation 1:14 speaks of Jesus' hair not in terms of Sallman's long, flowing locks but as *wool*. Canaanites *and* Hebrews had very curly hair. There are other words for this, but the point is that a historically accurate portrait would greatly assist African American children both to relate to Jesus and be proud of themselves, just like God made them.

Of course, there is ultimately no salvation in the physical features of any person. And we as African Americans can celebrate the Chinese Jesus painted by and for Chinese, the German Jesus of Sallman, painted by and for Germans, and the Native American artist who painted Jesus in the likeness of his own people. All complexions and physical features are just the envelopes inside of which are precious souls. And it's those souls that really count. The importance of even this message is not the advancement of any one color. Rather, we are focused on what thoughts about the outside do to the spiritual well-being of persons on the inside.

If, down deep, we are unhappy about our skin, our hair, or our facial features, we are at odds with the One who made them.

Spiritual wholeness requires that we be at peace with our Maker and ourselves. If, down deep, we are unhappy about our skin, our hair, or our facial features, we are at odds with the One who made them. We feel cheated by God and angry with life. We may hold this feeling in and try to hide it, but it will undermine our joy in the Lord and our own essential self-esteem. Therefore, without refusing to accept the appearance of any other group, for them, we simply must affirm how we look, for ourselves.

Another word from our text (Ps. 139:14) says it with proper gusto, "I will praise thee; for I am fearfully and wonderfully made." Real appreciation of how we are made is more than grudging tolerance or tight-jawed acceptance. Genuine gratitude pours forth in irresistible outbursts of praise to our Maker. Until there is a spontaneous, gut-level gladness about how we are made, we are still struggling against an undercurrent of self-hatred. It comes from the majority culture, which has taught us not to accept ourselves in the first place. But Jesus said the opposite. He surely didn't say "Don't love and accept yourself." He said love "thy neighbor as thyself " (Luke 10:27).

Real love draws out the praise and joy of the psalmist and of us as well. This is true regardless of whether it is our neighbor, our Creator, or ourselves whom we love. In fact, it must always be all three or none at all. Since it is so hard to let go and love self, let's look for some help in what might be called a parable of romantic love in a Christian marriage.

Nearly fifty years ago I gazed at my bride and saw a beauty in her that I had never seen before. True to stereotype, I tended to believe that she could never be that lovely again. But I was wrong; as the years rolled on, she became more and more lovely to these eyes. I was nearly moved to tears by her countenance as she approached the birth of a child. And the radiant face I saw when she nursed me through a critical illness made me burst forth daily in praise. I am teased for "not taking my eyes off her," even now, after just under fifty years. The point is that love and gratitude see real beauty, in the self as well as others. It causes hearty, irresistible praise.

Now, of course, we won't be praising our own looks that much, but to love one's own self fully is to see more and more of God's miracles right there in little old me. "I am awesomely and wonderfully made!" Unless we encourage and express this praise, we will never fully enjoy what God has given us. Love and praise that is inhibited and choked down dies for the lack of expression. And, strange as it may seem, the love and praise we should have for our very own selves is choked to death the same way: for our failure to express it to God and, yes, to ourselves.

It's like the savoring of a delicious dinner. If we gulp it down in a hurry and don't stop to enjoy the taste and wonder at the talents of the chef, we will miss much of the joy of the feast. If we don't stop to meditate and marvel at all God has done for us and with us, both inside and out, we will keep our crippling habits of low self-esteem. So our sincere praise is more for our benefit than anybody else's.

We were actually *made* for this purpose of praising God. We will find our greatest fulfillment in praising the Lord for what has been done in and for *us*, as well as for others.

During the great Civil Rights Revolution of the 1960s and 1970s, many African American young people changed their hair-styles to what is known as the "Afro." Some did it because they believed that this affirmed their identity and made a statement of self-esteem to the world. Others just followed along because it was the "in" thing to do. The style spread rapidly, and with no prece-dents or traditions for guides, it went to some extremes.

One young woman made the sacrifice and let her hair grow in wild profusion. She wanted to be accepted by the others on campus, but she longed for a visit to the old beauty shop, where they would "straighten" her hair. One day she saw a different kind of Afro. It was as natural as could be, but it was neatly trimmed, and it gave the woman who wore it a queenly elegance. Our friend just had to ask who had styled this hairdo. And she couldn't wait to get a style just like it.

The barber calmly informed her that he couldn't duplicate on her head the style he had given the other woman. He said he only *cut* hair, he didn't make it. But he thought she would probably like what he could do. She reluctantly said a faint Okay, and sat back nervously, almost tearfully, with her eyes shut. As the barber snipped, snipped, snipped away, she feared the worst. When she came in, she had at least a little bit of length, but now it sounded to her like he was cutting it all off. She was stiff as a board, and her jaws were tight, as she clutched the armrests for what seemed an eternity.

At last the ordeal was over. The barber handed her a mirror and told her to look it over. Quite hesitantly she opened her eyes and risked a "peek," first at the front and then at the back. Then suddenly she burst into tears. The barber was horrified, but quickly saw that these were tears of joy. She had never dreamed that an Afro could be such a halo to what she now saw as her lovely face. The brown hair framed a countenance she hadn't seen as pretty since she was a little girl. Even the barber felt a lump in his throat, to see how much happiness he had brought. She ran from mirror to mirror, screaming and jumping. She wanted to shout, like the old folks, but she didn't know how.

If she had only known the words, it would have been a perfect time to cry out with the psalmist and from the bottom of her soul: "I just have to praise you, Lord, because I am so awesomely and wonderfully fashioned by your hand. Everything you ever made is good, and that includes even me: Marvelous are your works! Oh, marvelous are your works! Yes, *Marvelous are your works; and that my soul knows right well! Hallelujah!*"

Questions for Discussion

The Skin I'm In

1. Read Jeremiah 13 (especially vv. 22-27). Why do you think God is using Ethiopians and leopards as examples? Do you think the first readers of this book saw the skin of the Ethiopian and the spots of the leopard positively or negatively? Why?

2. The Hebrew text could be translated, "*Will* the Ethiopian change his skin?" Have you heard of people changing the color of their skin? How is it done? Why is it done? Does it really make a difference?

3. Describe some of the beautiful and practical aspects of your skin. Identify three physical features that you like most about yourself. How do you feel about the skin you're in?

4. The message posits that humanity's obsession with skin is a result of sin. If this is the case, is it wrong to appreciate skin, or physical features? Can you think of a case wherein appreciation of the skin can be sinful? Why do people believe that Jesus rose from the dead in the skin?

5. Do you believe God made different groups of humans to look different? Why or why not? Read and discuss Acts 17:24-27; especially v. 26.

God's Handiwork: Me!

1. Have you ever praised God for the way you are made? State one thing about the way that you are made that makes you happy when you think about it.

2. Have you ever been ridiculed for the way you look? If so, describe the experience and how you felt about it.

3. Have you ever ridiculed others for the way they look? If so, describe the experience and try to remember why. How do you feel about it now?

4. What do you think about pressing and straightening hair? Is that a rejection of God's creative act? What about blue contact lenses? Skin lightening?

5. Read Revelation 1:13-15. If you were to see people today with physical features like those described in this text, in which ethnic group would you place them? Could they be Black people? Could they be White people? Why or why not? What does this discussion tell you about the identity of Jesus Christ? What does it say about your identity?

CHAPTER 5

Self-Esteem and
the Black Continent

Spicy grove, cinnamon tree,
What is Africa to me? [1]

he attitude of Black Americans toward Africa is ambiguous. Ranging from disinterest to Afrocentric celebration, Black people have widely differing feelings about the continent from which their ancestors came. Is America our homeland, or Africa? Do Black people here really have much in common with our African cousins beyond the color of our skins? To affirm our African roots, do we have to reject our American fruits? These and other questions often lie unanswered in the African American spirit.

This state of affairs is to be expected, given our education in the glories of European history. The average Black American has been taught Greek mythology instead of Egyptian mythology, European instead of African history, and has been groomed to exalt the art of White people over that of Black people. How can we take pride in that which we do not know?

The Bible is full of positive references to Africa, the land of Moses' birth, Israel's infancy, and Jesus' early childhood. Any Bible concordance reveals the names of great Africans like Hagar, Abraham's wife; Ebed-melech, Jeremiah's Ethiopian deliverer; Simon, Jesus' cross-sharer; and Queen Candace's Nubian treasurer. The preaching and teaching of texts like these can inspire Black people to embrace mother Africa and to esteem their own Africanness as a gift of God. The following sermons proclaim biblical affirmations of the blessings of Africa.

The Drama of a Daddy with a Dream

EMIL THOMAS

The angel of the Lord appeareth to Joseph in a dream, saying, Arise and take the young child and his mother, and flee into Egypt.

MATTHEW 2:13

Christmas is over, but the drama of redemption moves on. In our text, the shepherds had retired to their fields and flocks. The angels had returned to the celestial spheres. The star had retreated behind the black bosom of the cosmos. The wise men had departed to their own countries by an alternate route. Mary has her baby, and the earth has her Savior, but the drama moves on.

Approaching at center stage is a stepfather named Joseph. The sacred script suggests that he is provider and protector of his family. But how will he do it? He is a mere carpenter, a man of meager means. What can he do to care for the Christ-Child? He has no dollars, no domicile, and no degree. But he does have his dreams. And any daddy with the right dream can participate in the drama of redemption. In the dreams of this daddy are three scenes from the continuing drama of redemption.

Scene I

This daddy dreamed about deliverance from destruction. Joseph was minding his own business in Bethlehem. The wise men had left him a nest egg of gold, frankincense, and myrrh. Scholars say that the wise men probably arrived to see Jesus around two years after he was born. All of a sudden, Joseph has a dream. In it he hears a metaphysical message and an angelic announcement that he is to "Arise, and take the young child and his mother, and flee into Egypt, and be thou there until I bring thee word: for Herod will seek the young child to destroy him" (Matt. 2:13). It was in this dream that he found the key to deliverance from destruction.

Now he had been in Bethlehem for two years, but it took a dramatic dream to convince him that he was living in a dangerous situation. We should never get too comfortable where we live, because the "baddest" bullies can live in a good neighborhood. You see, Bethlehem was a good place to live, but there was a character named Herod who also lived there. Herod was mad with power. Herod ruled in Palestine for thirty-nine years. And Herod would do anything to keep his position. He killed his favorite wife, Mariamne, in 29 B.C. He killed two of his sons, Alexander and Aristobulus, in 7 B.C. In the last days of his life, he killed his first son, Antipater. Herod was hell-bent on eliminating every threat to his throne.

There are Herods still alive today, who will do anything to eliminate threats to their thrones. Herod will assassinate anyone with potential. Herod will kill John Kennedy and Bobby Kennedy. Herod will exile Marcus Garvey. Herod will kill Medgar Evers and murder Malcolm X. Herod will assign somebody to assassinate Martin Luther King, Jr. Herod will do anything to eliminate threats to his throne.

Black man, don't you know that you are a threat to Herod? Black woman, don't you know that your power makes Herod tremble in his boots? Don't you know that he doesn't want you to take his throne? You have already survived slavery. You have already built colleges and universities to educate your own. You have already fought the civil rights battles to obtain legal freedom in the land. You are already mayor of many major cities in this country. You already create the greatest music, culture, and art produced in the Western hemisphere. Your athletes are at the pinnacle of many sports. You are a threat to Herod's throne. He's got to get you out of the way. Herod will let drugs into his own country in order to destroy all threats. Herod will take banks and businesses out of your community and put liquor stores on every corner because he wants to destroy the threat. Herod will fill the jails with you to destroy the threat. Herod will put you in second-class schools to destroy the threat. Herod will go all the way to Africa to feed you if you're starving, but if you get a boat and come over from Haiti, Herod will let the boat sink before he lets you in.

The angel told Joseph, "Herod will seek the young child, to destroy him." Jesus was a threat. He was a born king. He had wise men seeking him out and stars shining in his favor. He already had Scriptures declaring that he would be born in Bethlehem. "I've got to kill him while he's still a child," reasoned Herod.

African American daddy, God wants you to protect your family from Herod. It is the noblest of traditions for the husband and wife to seek to share domestic responsibilities; but if you hear a noise in your house at night, it is not her job to go check it out—that is your job! For the Bible said in Ephesians 5:25, "Husbands, love your wives, even as Christ loved the church and gave himself for it." If one person has to die that the family might live, let it be daddy; not momma or baby!

"You take the young child, and Mary. Go on down to Egypt. Get on down to Africa and wait there until I bring you word." This idea was an inspired idea. Joseph could not think that up by himself. Joseph might have thought of going to Rome, the political capital of the world. He could have thought up Athens, in Greece, the philosophical headquarters of the Hellenistic world. He could have thought of Jerusalem, the religious capital of the world. But God's angel told him to go to Africa.

I have some ideas why. The first is theological, and the second is practical. Perhaps God wanted the second Adam to have some roots in Africa. In Genesis 2:11-13 the first two rivers mentioned in the Garden of Eden are in Africa; the rivers Pison and Gihon. The Pison goes through Havilah, which is Egypt. The Gihon encompasses the entire land of Ethiopia. Since Egypt and Ethiopia are in Africa, the first Adam was reared in Africa. I Corinthians 15:45 says that Jesus was the second Adam. The first Adam was a living soul; the second Adam is a life-giving Spirit. The first Adam was a natural man; the second Adam was a spiritual man. The first Adam is made from earth, the second Adam came from heaven.

The first Adam messed up the world; the second Adam mended the world. Jesus, the second Adam, had to undo what the first Adam had done. If the first Adam started the mess in Africa, then maybe the second Adam had to start the mending in Africa!

I wonder what Black Americans would do if the Lord told us to go to Africa?

But beyond that theological possibility there must have been a practical reason. Remember, Jesus found a hideout from Herod's destruction in Africa. When hiding someone, you don't hide them where they stick out, but where they blend in! I don't care how you wrap it up, bundle it up, and dress it up, you can't hide a blond-haired, blue-eyed baby in Harlem! It won't blend in—it will only stick out! Could it be that God willed it that Jesus would be hidden in Africa because with his physical features, he could blend right in? I wonder what Black Americans would do if the Lord told us to go to Africa? Though Jesus went to Africa, some of us are ashamed of the homeland of our ancestors. Though they are our kith and kindred, we don't even have adequate mission projects in Africa, as we leave that job to televangelists, relief organizations, and government agencies. We talk about the "old-time religion," but our religion is not old enough. It only goes back to "my old mother" and "my old father." It does not get back to Africa.

But Joseph did not shudder and shiver. Joseph did not shake and shirk his responsibility of the revealed dream. Joseph knew that not only did Adam live in Africa, but Moses was born in Africa. Hagar was born in Africa. Jacob's son Joseph, another dreamer, lived in Africa. He had a wife from Africa named Asenath, the daughter of Potiphera, priest of Heliopolis, who was the mother of Ephraim and Manasseh, two of the tribes of Israel. If Joseph had known the tune, he may have sung on his way to Africa, "Give me that old-time religion! Give me that old-time religion! If it was good enough for Moses, if it was good enough for Hagar, if it was good enough for Joseph, it's good enough for me!" When he took the family down to Africa, he set the stage for the prophecy to be fulfilled: "Out of Egypt have I called my son."

Scene II

This daddy's dream provided a detour around disaster. We see that the dream was correct in its prediction. After Herod found out that the wise men had not returned with the message of where the newborn king would be, he flew into a mad rage. So diabolical was his mind, that he ordered that every child two years old and under in Bethlehem and its environs should be killed. He would destroy all threats to his throne. No new kings would arise. No new queens would emerge. No new princes or princesses would appear in Bethlehem once they were all slain in childhood.

The Scriptures say that this also fulfilled the prophecy of Jeremiah 31:15: "A voice was heard in Ramah, lamentation, and bitter weeping; Rachel weeping for her children refused to be comforted, because they were not." Somebody heard a voice piercing the barriers of time. Somebody heard a sound that emanated from another dimension. Rachel, looking down on Bethlehem from the perspective of eternity, wept and wailed for the genocide and destruction of the children. Have you ever seen somebody cry and refuse to be comforted? Have you ever seen someone at a funeral weep for her child and refuse to be held by the ushers, deacons, and family members? Have you ever seen somebody say, "Turn me loose. If I don't cry today, the very rocks will cry out."

It has been some 2700 years now, but I can still hear Rachel weeping. That's a mighty long time, but Rachel refuses to cease her lamentations. Can't you hear her? Every time a child is born addicted to crack, can't you hear her cry? Every time a baby is born with AIDS and abandoned, can't you hear Rachel weeping? Can't you hear her weep when abandoned babies are found in dumpsters? Can't you hear her weep when a child is caught in the cross fire of a drive-by shooting, or when a child is struck down in gang violence, or when children are murdered for their tennis shoes or stadium jackets? I can even hear her weeping when young men sell drugs on corners, and youths drop out of high school. I can hear her weeping when young people don't have food to eat or a place to sleep. Oh yes! Rachel is still weeping.

But though Rachel is weeping, God is still speaking, and Joseph is still dreaming. "All day and all night, angels keep watching over me, my Lord." Joseph receives another angelic announcement that gives him an inspiring idea. "Arise, and take the young child and his mother and go into the land of Israel, for they are dead which sought the young child's life." You see, Herods have a problem— they all die after a while. I don't care how efficient their evil or how tyrannical their reign, they, too, must give up the ghost. Rachel, don't you weep, don't you moan, though evil is everywhere, even Herod must die after a while.

Joseph takes Jesus and Mary and heads back to the land of Israel. But notice, the dream was not specific. *Where* in Israel should he go? Sometimes the drama of life, the dreams that we have require us to march without a map, not knowing exactly where God will lead us, but we must walk by faith, and not by sight.

It seems that Joseph was heading back to Bethlehem. He had been established himself there, and now is preparing to return. But before he arrives, he hears some disturbing and disconcerting news. Herod is dead, but Archelaus, his son, rules in his stead. Herod has left a son to sit in his place, and continue his policies.

A daddy with no spiritual discernment would say that a new day was dawning, because Herod was dead. But Archelaus was only a new and improved version of Herod. He did everything that Herod did, but he was more slick, smooth, and subtle. Herod was a murderer, but Archelaus was a manipulator. Herod was violent, but Archelaus was vicious. Herod was a thief, but Archelaus was an embezzler. Herod was a drunkard, but Archelaus was a substance abuser. Herod was a liar, but Archelaus was a reinterpreter of the truth. Herod was a straight-up whoremonger, but Archelaus was a pimpish playboy. I tell you, Archelaus was slick, smooth, and subtle!

As African Americans, we are not so threatened by the hellish hatred of Herod, but by the artistic avarice of Archelaus. We in Black America need to recognize that even though Herod is dead,

Archelaus is ruling in his stead. Herod always leaves an Archelaus behind to continue his work. That is why Herod killed Alexander, Aristobulus, and Antipater. They were too independent. But he let Archelaus live. The others were his sons, but Archelaus was his *boy.*

Herod will send an assassin—Archelaus will send you an award.

Archelaus has the same agenda, spirit, and program as Herod: to eliminate all threats to his throne. But Archelaus has a different *modus operandi.* Herod will kill you—Archelaus will co-opt you. Herod will send an assassin—Archelaus will send you an award. Herod will massacre you early on, but Archelaus will massage your ego. Herod seeks to destroy you with segregation—Archelaus will just dilute you with integration. Herod will fire you, but Archelaus will hire you. Herod kills the body, but Archelaus kills the brain. Herod kills the man, but Archelaus just kills the mind. Both of them end up eliminating you as a threat to the throne.

Some of us as Black folk have escaped the mass destruction of Herod only to become mental disasters under Archelaus. I don't know about you, but I'd rather see a Black man or woman suffer a premature death under Herod than to live only to be brainwashed by Archelaus.

You can always tell when Archelaus has gotten to one of our brothers or sisters. Have you ever seen a brother who has a car but won't give anybody a ride? Archelaus got him! Have you ever seen a sister who has money but won't give anyone a loan? Archelaus got her! Have you ever seen an African American who has a position of power but won't give a young brother or sister a job? Archelaus has got them!

Some African Americans get happy when right-wing politicians get voted out of office, because we think that means that Herod is dead. But we must remember that before Herod leaves, he always puts Archelaus in place. You see, Archelaus can be Democrat or Republican. Archelaus can be liberal or conservative. Archelaus' skin can be snow white or jet black. Learn from the dreams of this daddy. After you dodge the destruction of Herod, make sure you detour around the disaster of Archelaus.

Scene III

The dream of this daddy facilitated Christ's date with destiny. God kept on speaking, and Joseph kept on dreaming. He received another inspired idea. This time God showed up. When you deal with the destruction of Herod, God can send an angel. When it comes to dealing with the disaster of Archelaus, God can send an angel. But when it comes to getting you to your date with destiny, God has to show up in person. If God doesn't show up, Archelaus may delay your development. Archelaus may cause you to miss your appointment. Archelaus can get you sidetracked on self. So God showed up in person. I can imagine the conversation.

"Joseph, I know that you like the sweet suburbs of Bethlehem. I know that you are dreaming of raising your family in the cultural context of Judea. But remember, Joseph, Jesus is your adopted child, but he's my only begotten Son! Take him on up to Nazareth! I know that the school system is bad there, but take him there anyway. I know that there is not much Jewish culture there, but take him there anyway. I know that it is parochial and provincial—I know there is crime and violence up there in the ghettos of Galilee—and I know that Nazareth is not known for producing greatness. But when you get back from Africa, just take my boy up to Nazareth."

I can hear Joseph saying, "But Lord, it's mighty dark up there."

But the Lord said, "The people in darkness need to see a great light."

"But Lord, there is death, destruction, and disaster in the slums and projects of Nazareth."

"I know that, but it is upon them that sit in the very shadow of death that the light must shine."

So Joseph took his family and relocated in Nazareth. Whenever you follow God's dream, prophecy is fulfilled. If he had stayed in Bethlehem, Jesus may have been called a "wannabe." If he had stayed with Archelaus, he may have been called an Uncle Tom. But Jesus made his date with destiny, and today we call him "the Man from Nazareth." After getting Jesus to Nazareth we hear of Joseph no more. He exited stage left, turning the drama of redemption over to the main character, the star of human history, the Man from Nazareth.

But the curtain does not close! The drama continued! The Man from Nazareth was baptized by John in the Jordan! The Man from Nazareth preached the gospel to the poor and fed the hungry! The Man from Nazareth healed the sick and raised the dead! The Man from Nazareth opened blinded eyes, unstopped deaf ears and cut loose stammering tongues! The Man from Nazareth was hung on a cross one Friday. He gave his hands to the nails, his feet to the spikes, and his side to the spear. He gave forgiveness to his enemies—he gave salvation to a thief—he gave his mother to John, and he gave John to his mother! The Man from Nazareth hung his head on his shoulder and gave his spirit to God. He died!

It seemed as if the drama was over. The sun protested the apparent end of the episode and refused to shine. The black velvet curtain of eternity dropped on the stage at Calvary. The earth experienced an epileptic seizure, and vomited up some of its dead. But when Jesus is on stage, the show is never over! Three days later, early on Sunday morning, the drama continued! The curtain rose, and someone was standing at center stage! Someone in the audience said, "Who is this that comes from Edom with dyed garments of Bozrah? Who is that, so glorious in his apparel, standing in the greatness in his strength?"

Somebody else said, "I don't know, but he looks like the Man from Nazareth! Hush! He's getting ready to speak."

The crowd hushed. His mouth opened, and his tongue spoke. *"All power in heaven and earth has been given into my hands! Let the drama of redemption continue!"*

The Roots of the Spirit

HENRY H. MITCHELL

But let your heartfelt confidence be in the Lord; and always be ready to give an answer to everyone who asks you to explain why you have such hope, but be sure to answer in humility and respect.

I PETER 3:15 AP

Perhaps the most damaging accusation aimed at us who are African American Christians is that we got our religion from the White man. Black nationalists who are not believers will swear that our faith was given to us, word for word, to make us better slaves. Now this is partly true, in that the slave masters did try to use the Bible that way. So what do we say to offset this quarter truth and witness with convicting power to our African American Christian faith? How do we justify our coherent joy in Jesus?

The apostle Peter suggests an answer or strategy in his letter to Christians who were under attack. The Greco-Roman world oppressed Christians, not only by violence but by arguments and propaganda. They were accused of being ignorant upstarts. Peter, who was not formally trained (he had Silas write for him), wisely advised persecuted Christians to have a good understanding of their faith. It wasn't that he thought one could argue another out of her or his faith; it was simply very important to be able to testify so clearly that anybody could see that the Christian faith made sense.

Peter said, in effect, "Be prepared to answer any of these false charges made against you. Show them that your faith is at least as reasonable or coherent as theirs." His exact words included three admonitions. The first was to have complete confidence in Christ, above all human ideas. One wouldn't need a defense unless one had such a faith in Christ in the first place.

The last of the three was an admonition to keep humble, even though one's reasonable answers could embarrass persecutors. In a word, don't put them down, just because you know your arguments so well and can rebut the critics so easily.

African Americans must first answer with hard data about the African roots of their belief system.

The middle admonition in this verse is the one we want to work with today: have an answer that demonstrates that the Christian faith makes good sense. Once a person believes, there is no problem getting this faith to fit with reality. All other belief systems have the same challenge; none can *prove* itself "true." All people can do is testify that it works for them, and that it fits together.

In other words, learn how to explain calmly what you believe and why—to respond to every question and testify gladly. And this advice from Peter is very wise in our situation as African American Christians.

Peter himself answered false charges and mockings point blank, with facts and no apologies: "You people of Judaea, and all y'all that live in Jerusalem, listen to me: This which you see was spoken by the prophet Joel" (Acts 2:14 and 16). When he was finished with a long quotation from Joel, he then proceeded to present Jesus also as fulfilling prophecy.

Likewise, African Americans must first answer with hard data about the African roots of their belief system. One fact is that Africans have been believers since the very beginning of human history. No slave master taught us to believe. In fact, dark skinned Ethiopians were among the first to worship and, thus, taught all their succeeding generations to believe in the afterlife, and to worship God.

All human bones are distinguished from anthropoid ape bones by the tools and artifacts in the graves. Tools prove that the bones belonged to thinkers, or *homo sapiens* (man the thinker). But they wouldn't have put the tools in graves in the first place if they hadn't also been *homo credens* (man the believer) in an afterlife and in a Deity.

The critics who charge that African American Christians got their faith from Whites bent on making better slaves need to know another historic fact: enslaved Africans virtually stole the Bible from masters, who would not let slaves read the Bible. And there were far too few clergy to give serious attention to saving slaves, who may not have been thought to have souls anyway. The slaves therefore interpreted the Bible their own way. Otherwise, how could they have sung, "Go down, Moses, . . . Tell ol' Pharaoh to let my people go." The "Invisible Institution" or independent underground religion of slaves is the mother of the Christianity of the Black masses.

It may appear strange to critics that their African American slave ancestors should have taken to the Bible and the Christian faith so readily. But here, again, the apostle Peter's principle applies. Peter made it plain that he was in accord with history and tradition. There was nothing radically new about his preaching at Pentecost. It was merely the fulfillmment of previous prophecy. And this is exactly what happened with African Traditional Religion (ATR). Its best tenets were affirmed and fulfilled in Christianity.

For instance, the theology or doctrine of our African ancestors (ATR) was expressed in "Praise-Names" for God. These traits of The Most High God of the Africans are little different from the traits or characteristics of the Hebrews' Jehovah. Indeed the monotheistic faith and tribal culture of our West African ancestors were amazingly close to the early culture of Israel. Both believed in only one God. The primary difference was that Olorun of the Yorubas (Nigeria) had many deputy deities, a bureaucratic monotheism. And Olorun was even more transcendent than Elohim of the Hebrews.

Far from deserving to be thought of as heathen, our ancestors had complex ideas about God. The Yoruba's Olodumare was and is exactly what we mean when we say Almighty God. The Akan praise name for God as Omniscient was and is Brekyirihunuade. Their High God meted out justice and was both omnipresent and transcendent. These names all state in concrete characteristics what many books on theology might seek to portray.

So African American Christianity is far more African in spirit than our critics would allow. We have brought from home our own belief system, our own pattern of dealing with Holy Writ, our own way of preaching, and our own way of worship. Indeed, our faith has its roots in Africa, not Europe. And our religion is the most African thing we as a people have in this "New World." We are truly Christian, since we accepted Jesus and the printed Bible so completely, but we are also authentically and unashamedly African. How dare anyone say that we bought someone else's religion!

Following Peter's rules of reason or credibility, and applying them to his sermon at Pentecost, we find yet another use of tradition: to support a major breakthrough. Here at Pentecost was a strange and apparently new phenomenon to them; the Holy Spirit was manifest in dramatic ways. But even the power of God likely would not have been acceptable without Peter's long and verbatim quotation from the prophet Joel.

He said that God had promised to pour out the Holy Spirit on all flesh. If this seemed strange to those watching it happen at Pentecost, this was not unusual. If one had not seen such a thing before, one would not know exactly what to expect, even though one might believe Joel's prophecy. This was why Peter had to defend against the charge that they at Pentecost were full of wine and drunk, rather than full of the joy of the Holy Spirit. The sermon on prophecy helped overcome resistance.

Our African American ancestors had none of the Jerusalem church's problems in trying to understand the works of the Holy Spirit. Ever since the very first gatherings of Africans for worship, they were possessed by the spirits, even when they had to sneak away in order to practice their faith. What was looked on by Whites as frenzy took on a new name, shouting and praising God, in the power of the one Holy Spirit.

When the White folks had a nationwide revival called the First Great Awakening, they too began to shout. This was so much like home that the slaves joined the Christian churches by the thousands. As new Christians, some, though not all, could now worship with the approval of the masters. Some even were allowed to worship with their masters, from special seats. The Christian belief system was already parallel to their roots, and now this free and spontaneous worship simply sealed the bond.

So Peter's advice about being able to explain our African American Christian faith to our questioners and critics can be followed with ease. But there is one more great basis for faith that Peter's kinfolks would have cited then, and they rejoice in it even now: the Exodus. It was the Exodus from slavery in Egypt that revealed to the Hebrews who Jehovah really was. We African

Americans have our own brand of Exodus, and we knew who God was long before we were delivered. This meets one last question and challenge from the critics and also from seeking unbelievers.

They wonder why, if God is like we say God is, we should ever have had to face all this injustice through these 350 years. They say they don't blame the Jews for believing in God, because they believe God delivered them from slavery. They had their Exodus. But they feel that God has abandoned African Americans—if indeed there is a God.

Now we all know that God doesn't have to answer these critics, but the apostle Peter suggests that we believers ought to be able to give an answer even so. And we African Americans just happen to have an Exodus of our own. Just as surely as God delivered the Jews from Pharaoh in Egypt, God delivered our ancestors from slavery in America. And God is still working beyond our human limits to overcome injustice and oppression.

Lincoln did not in fact free the slaves.

One way to explain how we know that God freed the slaves is by carefully reading the facts behind the history. In the first place, Lincoln did not in fact free the slaves. His Emancipation Proclamation was a military strategy, to help undermine the slave labor support of the South's rebels. Actually it only declared freedom in the seceding states, leaving our ancestors in chains in Kentucky and parts of Virginia.

Again, some might think that the military forces of the North freed the slaves, but this is quite to the contrary. The great city of New York had draft riots and lynchings and burnings, because the citizens there resented going to a war that they perceived as being waged to stop slavery. Unwilling White soldiers resorted to the cover of "friendly fire" to shell their own Black troops up front, supposedly by accident.

Others might credit the Abolitionists with having had much to do with the abolition of slavery. But they were too few and had too little power and influence to be taken seriously or to turn the tide of history.

To put it very plainly, only God delivered the slaves, and this would have happened no matter which side won the bloody war. Less than a month before the surrender of the South, they had run so short of recruits that they voted to enlist African American slaves. And they were well aware that they could no longer call wives and parents and children slaves, when these men had guns and live ammunition. The cruel institution of slavery was over, regardless.

When the surrender of the South had been formalized, Lincoln walked up Broad Street in Richmond, Virginia, and made a speech from the steps of the capitol. He declared to the jubilant newly freed, "You are free. You are free as any man. Let none tell you that you are not free. *God has set you free!*" This statement emerged from his usual honesty and complete candor. He knew well that it was not his primary goal, nor could any other man or woman take credit.

The ex-slaves cheered and cheered, but they knew well that he was telling the truth. They said it this way: "*Marse Lincum sign de paper, but Gawd de one what sot us free!*"

Nobody sat down and taught those old sisters and brothers to read history that well, and certainly no master taught them how to praise God for their deliverance from slavery. It was their own interpretation of the Bible and their own deep faith in God that gave them their marvelously accurate insights. And this is part of the reason why so many African Americans confess faith in God as revealed in Jesus Christ. Nobody else gave us our faith; we got it from God and from our ancestors. This is what our people have been saying for centuries, even long before the slave trade.

Then hear, Oh you critics, and you that call faith in Jesus Christ "a white man's religion."

We serve the God of the Bible and of our ancestors.

We first heard of Jesus from white people, but we found out for ourselves that he was a Liberator of both body and soul.

We sing about Jesus from the manger to the cross, but we sing about him with our own stirring songs.

We trust in a God of justice, but only our ancestors, not our masters, could have told us about this side of God.

We love to recite the Bible verse by verse, but we ourselves interpret what it means with the help of God.

We know, like our Hebrew brethren, that God can break the chains asunder and set the captives free.

We know, like our ancestors, that death is not the end and that there is another home on the other side.

But we know that God is still working on this side, until the whole world is one extended family of love and justice.

So no critic can turn us back now; we've come too far through too many storms with too much faith to turn back now.

And now may the God of Abraham, Isaac, and Jacob,
of Kunta Kente and his grandma, Yaisa,
of Deborah and Priscilla, of Harriet and Sojourner,
of Crispus and Frederick, of Martin and Malcolm,
the God of *all* our mothers and fathers,
that God revealed supremely in our Lord Jesus Christ—
may *that* God strengthen your roots and enlighten your mind,
and give you love and power, peace and joy! Amen!

Questions for Discussion

The Drama of a Daddy with a Dream

1. Jesus' stay in Africa fulfilled the prophecy about Israel, "Out of Egypt have I called my son." Read Matthew 2:15, Hosea 11:1, and Exodus 4:22. What do these verses mean to you?
2. Egypt is often viewed as the source of Western Civilization. What color were the ancient Egyptians? What was the texture of their hair? Where did you get your information?
3. The sermon proposed that the garden of Eden was in Africa. Read Genesis 2:10-14. What is your idea?

4. What other reasons can you give for God's sending of Jesus to Africa? Why didn't God send Jesus to Europe? To Asia?
5. The sermon suggests Jesus may have lived in a Black community in Africa, and a "bad" community in Nazareth. What is it like to live in a community of Black people? A "bad" community? Is there any relation between the two?

The Roots of the Spirit

1. The sermon advises us to put Christ "above all human ideas." What "human ideas" were you taught about Africa?
2. Do you believe that you have roots in Africa? How do you know that you do or you don't? Are you proud of your roots? If so, how do you show it?
3. This sermon gives evidence that God has been active in African American history. Do you see evidence of God in the history of Black people today? Where? Do you see evidence of God in African events today? Where?
4. African slaves accepted Christianity. Today, some Black people reject Christianity as a "white man's religion." Why do you think this is? What is your position?
5. What African history have you studied? Where can you get more information about African history, culture, and religion? Do you plan to do so?

CHAPTER 6

Self-Esteem
and Black Capacity

*Have your own newspapers, have your own artists, have your own
sculptors, have your own pulpits, . . . print your own books and show
your own motion pictures . . . Glorify all the good in yourselves.*

Marcus Garvey[1]

n appalling percentage of African Americans are convinced that they and all their ethnic kin are limited in
intelligence. They refuse to patronize African American lawyers, physicians, and other professionals and
businesses. When they hear of failures or conflicts in their churches
or communities, their all-purpose explanation is, "Well, you know
how we are." It never occurs to them that their kinfolk have passed
the same tests as people of other groups. They seem never to hear
of a Ben Carson, M.D., who grew up in the worst kind of ghetto,
yet became perhaps the nation's most distinguished neurosurgeon;
or a May Jemison, M.D., who was sent into space to do research.
They manage to support their judgment by seeing only what
appears to confirm it. Mass media compound their problem by
projecting largely White models of excellence.

This is more than a psychological problem. To believe in
race-wide disabilities is, consciously or unconsciously, to blame the
Creator who made them. Strong preaching on the equality of the
gifts of God is therefore both sound doctrine and good therapy.

The prejudiced appraisal of the keystone or "chief of the corner," in Matthew 21:42-44 is Jesus' response to the similarly prejudiced evaluation accorded him by the oppressors of church and empire. He who "was acquainted with our grief" clearly suggested that God, who assigns gifts and positions in life, can place the despised and rejected at the top of the arch. And those who disregard him can stumble over the stone and be made to fall. Thus, "The Cornerstone Conspiracy" speaks to the desperate need for self-esteem among African Americans.

Part of the low self-evaluation of African Americans can be traced to a much too limited concept of what real wisdom is. All too often, wisdom is confused with formal training, which is still in short supply among the oppressed minorities of America. Yet it has been true, ever since the first slave landed, that oppressors were happy to recognize gifts of African Americans if they could control and profit from them. "Wisdom Redefined" is designed to broaden sensitivity to true wisdom, and to increase African American awareness of God's gifts to them.

The Cornerstone Conspiracy

EMIL THOMAS

Jesus saith unto them, Did ye never read in the scriptures, The stone which the builders rejected, the same is become the head of the corner: this is the Lord's doing, and it is marvelous in our eyes? Therefore, say I unto you, The kingdom of God shall be taken from you , and given to a nation bringing forth the fruits thereof. And whosoever shall fall on this stone shall be broken: but on whomsoever it shall fall, it will grind him to powder.

MATTHEW 21:42-44

In Matthew 21, Jesus painted a picture about builders, architects, and contractors. Allow your mind to be the canvas and for your imagination to give life to the portrait. Can't you just see them as they plan to build a building? Can you imagine them beginning to select their building materials? Indeed, materials that will be used in the building process are crucial to the quality of the project. They need some wood in the superstructure, some metal in the infrastructure, and they need some stone to undergird the total structure. So from the forest they select the finest wood. From the mines they extract the most durable metals. They hasten to the quarries to select the most important element, the stone—for without a stone foundation, the infrastructure and superstructure are liable to fall. Those stones that they like, they take with them. But those they don't are cast on the junk heap. They are careful and cautious, most deliberate in their decisions. As a matter of fact, before they leave, they notice a stone among their selections that doesn't fit their liking. "What is this doing here?" they ask. "Throw it out! we don't need that one!" So they cast it on the scrap heap, toss it on the junk pile, and leave the quarry, to commence with their building. I wonder why they reject it? Do they consider it to be of inferior quality? Do they think it is the wrong color? Maybe they think that it is a stone of the wrong shape, or size, or strength. But whatever the case, they conclude that it is not the right kind of stone for the building they have in mind. So they reject that stone. Hidden among the scraps and piled on top of junk, it is forsaken and forgotten.

But now look at them! With all of their materials selected, they begin their building. Before long, however, they reach an impasse. When the time comes to place the cornerstone, the most important stone to support the infrastructure and superstructure, none of their selections quite fit. They search and search among the stones that they had selected, but none of them will work. They now go back to the quarry to try to purchase one that will meet their needs, but nothing will suffice. But as they leave the quarry, they happen to pass by the scrap heap, and a marvel meets their eyes. Hidden within the refuse and rubbish of the junk pile is the ideal stone. And lo and behold, it is the same stone that they had scrapped just a few days before. They take it, and strategically place it in the structure. Not just in the corner, but at the head of the corner. It becomes the chief cornerstone. The very stone which the builders rejected becomes the chief cornerstone!

Jesus paints this proverbial picture in our imagination to high-light one of the problems of this world. For in this life, for some reason, people tend to ignore the essential, misplace the central, and discard what is most crucial. For some reason, people will scrap the best and embrace the worst. They will exile excellence to the junk heap and give their all for the mediocre. It is the cause of much pain and frustration. It is the cause of much hurt, harm, and danger. It wouldn't be so bad if it were an accident. But the text says that the action of the builders was deliberate and intentional. It is not basically a case of mistake, malfunction, or malfeasance. It is not simply a case of ignorance, innocence, or insensitivity. It cannot be excused as a missed opportunity or a case of mistaken identity. For this is done by people who are knowledgeable and informed about building materials. It is done by professional build-ers. The scripture does not say, "the stone which the builders misplaced." Nor does it say, "the stone which the builders forgot." But it does say, "the stone which the builders *rejected.*" It is in reality a rejection. It is a plot and a plan. It is deliberate! It is intentional! It is a conspiracy! I call it "The Cornerstone Conspir-acy."

In this life it is possible to be rejected, not because you are the worst, but because you are the best.

The cornerstone conspiracy has some *individualistic implications.* In other words, in this life, every individual ought to be prepared to cope with, to confront, and to creatively combat the cornerstone conspiracy. If you are not prepared to be its victor, you may become its victim.

In this life it is possible to be rejected, not because you are the worst, but because you are the best. In each mention of this parable in three Gospels (and in the psalms) there is never the slightest suggestion that there was any defect in the stone. It must have been a strong stone, because it was placed at the head of the corner. It must have been a sturdy stone, if it were to be used to support the rest of the building. It must have been a strikingly attractive stone, if it was to be of capstone or cornerstone quality. As a matter of fact, sound logic suggests that it must have been a mighty good stone, an excellent stone of superior quality. But instead of being selected, it was rejected. Instead of being picked, it was panned. Instead of being embraced and exalted, it was expunged and eliminated. The failure was not in the stone, but in the folk who evaluated the stone!

Likewise, in life, individuals can be rejected not in spite of, but because of their gifts, talents, and capacities. Marcus Garvey was not exiled from this country because he did not have organizational, administrative, and leadership skills, but because he did. The Daughters of the American Revolution did not reject Marian Anderson from a chance to sing in their facilities because she couldn't sing, but because she could! Thurgood Marshall was not barred from admission to the University of Maryland Law School because he wasn't intelligent, but because he was! Satchel Paige was not refused admission into the major leagues because he couldn't pitch, but because he could! Adam Clayton Powell was not censured by the congress because he was not a politician's politician, but because he was! Nelson Mandela was not put in jail because he had no leadership ability, but because he did! Winnie Mandela was not prosecuted because she had no integrity, but because she did! The failure was not in the stone, but in the folk who evaluated the stone!

Don't think that because you were not hired it necessarily follows that you are not qualified. It may be that you are just not the right kind of stone that the employer was looking for! Don't think that just because you weren't promoted that you don't have the capacities to move up. It may be that you are just what the company needs, but maybe your boss is threatened by you! Don't think that because you were not elected president of your auxiliary that you are not the most able person there. It may be that the whole group has pledged itself to a conspiracy of mediocrity, and they don't want you to raise the standard! Don't think that they didn't give you the solo because you can't sing. It may be that they don't want anyone to know that you can hit a higher note than they can! Be humble, be excellent, and don't "become weary in doing good, for at the proper time we will reap a harvest, if we do not give up" (Gal. 6:9 NIV).

The worst thing that can happen to individuals when rejected is that they will accept that rejection as a just verdict against their own self-worth. They can fall into self-doubt, self-pity, and even self-flagellation. For when you do that, you become a hapless coconspirator with those who rejected you in the first place. And when your enemies have you fighting yourself, their victory over you is sweet indeed. But in order to creatively confront the cornerstone conspiracy, you must know yourself and your soul. You must have a healthy and wholesome love of your God-given soul that transcends the appraisals, opinions, and evaluation of others, and that is even deeper than the natural talents and spiritual gifts that you possess.

The cornerstone conspiracy also has *racial ramifications*. In the building of this nation, in the construction of this country, there is a conspiracy afoot. It is a conspiracy to write off whole races from the blueprint of history. It is a conspiracy to relegate minorities to the scrap heap of insignificance. It is a conspiracy to banish entire peoples to the junk piles of civilization. The builders of Western culture are rejecting entire races that are cornerstone material.

If you focus on the person who rejects you, you give him or her power over you.

How can a race of people respond to such systematic rejection? The text says that "the stone that the builders rejected *has become* the chief cornerstone." You see, the cornerstone was a cornerstone wherever it was. It had the innate qualities of a cornerstone. It was cornerstone material. Whether it was on the scrap heap, the junk pile, or in the structure of the building, it was still cornerstone material. It did not have to act like a cornerstone. It did not have to prove that it was a cornerstone. It did not have written upon it that it was a corner-stone. It was essentially and innately a cornerstone. It did not have to *do* anything to prove it was a cornerstone. The answer was not in *doing* but in *being*.

Sometimes, I believe that some Black people give too much credit to White people as oppressors and arbiters of their destiny. If we focus on people who reject us, we give them power over us. If we spend all of our psychic energy worrying about the rejection of the builders or even trying to compensate for the misinformation perpetuated about us by the builders, we will not have the time to *be* who we are! No one but God is the final arbiter of our destiny! Our very survival is evidence that we must be cornerstone material! Yes, we were stolen from the Gold Coast of Africa. Yes, we were chained and bound for the perilous journey of the Middle Passage. Yes, we were subjected to the taskmaster's lash and inhuman bondage of chattel slavery—but we're still here! Yes, our women were abused, men psychologically damaged, and families dismantled—but we're still here! Yes, we were subjected to a century of legal segregation, deprived of the right to vote, left out of the history books, and made out to be the pariahs of a decadent moral order—but we're still here! God has given us some cornerstone capabilities!

I have always loved the New York Giants. But a few years ago I was shocked to learn that they had put O. J. Anderson on waivers. The builders of the team said that he was getting old. They said that they had to build the franchise on younger players. They wanted someone who was more thrilling and exciting for the fans, who would spin and fake and juke while he ran. But O. J. would just hit the hole time after time, and make that short, dependable yardage. The owners of the team seemed unimpressed that he had led the team in rushing the last few years, and that he almost never fumbled the ball. So they put him on waivers, which is to say, "If any other team wants him, come and get him."

As he languished on the scrap heap of time and age, no other team seemed to want him. So the Giants went back and picked him up one more time. It so happened, that O. J. Anderson became the hub of the offense that year. I watched him take them all the way to the Super Bowl. They were playing the Buffalo Bills, who had a brilliant lineup of players, both in the trenches and in the "skills positions." But whenever the Giants handed it to O. J. Anderson, he didn't try to do the impossible. He just did what he could do. He hit the hole and made his yardage. As a matter of fact, they won the game, and who did they name as the most valuable player? O. J. Anderson!

I said to myself, "The Scripture has been fulfilled in some measure today, for the stone which the builders rejected has become the chief of the corner. This is the Lord's doing, and it is marvelous in our eyes."

Stop worrying about what the other team is doing. Stop trying to imitate the style of other folk who are in the game. Maybe God didn't give you a spin, a fake, and a juke. But don't worry about that. When you get the ball just hit the hole and make your yardage! The outcome of the game is in God's hands!

The cornerstone conspiracy has *christological connotations*. That's right! This conspiracy is deeper than its implications for the individual and its ramifications in the racial arena. Supremely and superbly, this proverb is a picture of Christ!

Don't fool yourself. Because you are important to your auxiliary, you may be *a* cornerstone; but are not *the* Cornerstone! Being a powerful patriarch or a mighty matriarch in your family may make you *a* cornerstone; but it does not make you *the* Cornerstone! Being an organizing member of your church may have put your name on your *church* cornerstone, but don't ever confuse yourself with the *Chief* Cornerstone! Yes, Black people have scientific foundations for claiming cornerstone status as the first human beings. But remember that Christ, the Cornerstone of the cosmos, is the Creator and Redeemer of all humankind! Jesus Christ is the Cornerstone *par excellence!*

He is the foundation for the infrastructure of the universe and the superstructure of the human race. He is the Beginning and Ending of history, the Author and Finisher of our faith, and the Alpha and Omega of all being. But when he appeared in human history, he was despised and rejected. He came unto his own and his own received him not. He was constantly rejected by his own creation and relegated to the periphery of their attention. But no matter where he was or how people viewed him, he continued to be who he was, the Chief Cornerstone!

Many people have centered their hope in their psychology. They come to church for a psychological boost on Sunday. A lot of people have centered their hopes in their sociology. They are Afrocentric, ethnocentric, and Egyptocentric. All of that is fine, but these will all falter if they are not Christocentric! Without Christ, your individualistic psychology can become a feel-good religion that tickles the itching ear without saving the sin-sick soul! Without Christ, faith may melt down into a cult of self-improvement that falls short on self-sacrifice, self-criticism, or self-denial. But if you follow Jesus and deny yourself, you will not only discover yourself—you will transcend and fulfill yourself!

It's all right to take up a Kente cloth, a red, black, and green flag, sport an African name, and wear dreadlocks. But Jesus said, "take up your cross and follow me." I tell you, there is far more redemptive power in Christ than in your culture! If you want to handle this conspiracy well, you've got to follow the man who confronted the conspiracy, and conquered the conspiracy! His name is Jesus!

> My hope is built on nothing less
> Than Jesus' blood and righteousness.
> I dare not trust the sweetest frame,
> But wholly lean on Jesus' name.
>
> On Christ the Solid Rock I stand,
> All other ground is sinking sand;
> All other ground is sinking sand.[2]

Wisdom Redefined

HENRY H. MITCHELL

That Christ may dwell in your hearts by faith; and that you, being rooted and grounded in love, may be able to sense and understand with all saints what is the breadth, and length, and depth, and height; and to know the love of Christ, which is even better than academic and scientific knowledge.

EPHESIANS 3:17-18 (AP)

Of all the reasons we as African Americans have for thinking so little of ourselves, the most devastating may very well be the fact that we see ourselves as ignorant—mentally inferior, just plain dumber than the other races. On the job, in school, wherever—except in sports and show business—we know before we start that we can't compete. And so we chain ourselves to our own low level of expectation. It's like saying to teachers, preachers, and parents who expect more of us, "Get off my back! Can't you see I'm Black? Don't you know I'm inferior?"

I want to offer a new definition for wisdom, taken from Paul's letter to the church at Ephesus. It was written at a time when Greeks had the notion that their wisdom and their culture in general were vastly superior to all others. Paul's main concern was for Christians to be filled with the fullness of God, but wisdom was deeply involved, as you will see.

Before I begin to deal with the text's wisdom, I feel led to deal with the opposite, ignorance. What *is* ignorance? What comes to your mind when you hear that word? At first you are probably thinking "illiterate," or some other word for little or no formal education, in grammar school or anywhere else. Wrong! In our culture it is very important to be able to read, but let me remind you how many truly great people didn't read.

Our African family tree is loaded with people like the griot who recited history for seven days to Alex Haley, and never ever repeated himself or made a mistake. With a computerlike memory, you hardly *needed* to read in that culture. Whole villages of the griot's neighbors and relatives knew the history almost as well as he. You wouldn't dare call *any* of those people ignorant, regardless of reading skills.

The African Methodist Episcopal denomination was organized in 1816, with a young son of Bishop Allen serving as clerk, because he could read and write. Their first college-trained bishop was elected in 1880. Thus, the great leadership of our early churches was *wise* but not formally educated.

But we should have known this from even earlier evidence. The disciples of Jesus did not write either, with the possible exceptions of Matthew and maybe Judas. Peter's Epistles were dictated to Silas, or Silvanus, who could write. Fisherman Peter apparently could not.

I know you're saying, "But isn't illiteracy a curse?" Well, it may be a terrible handicap in our day of free education, but it isn't a curse. It is an inconvenience that can and should be overcome. It is an embarrassment, as it was for my teenage driver when he had to wake me up because he couldn't even read a street sign. Or when a preacher at a national conference agreed to read the Scripture, only to stumble all the way through a familiar passage. He was not cursed by his limitations; he was disgraced by his obvious lies about not having his glasses.

Remember, it is better to carry your Bible under your arm *and* in your heart. But if you had to choose only one, it would have to be the heart. Print is a substitute for memory, not memory a substitute for print. The Bible itself was first passed around in what we call "oral tradition," *then* written down and later printed.

So now what is Paul saying about true wisdom? How would he define it? Clearly he is saying that the highest knowledge is of the love of Christ, which surpasses secular learning and knowledge. Not that it cancels school learning, but it fulfills the true ends of learning. The best of secular learning is empty without the love of Christ. And this is learned in the *giving and receiving* of human love, not in schools and libraries.

It is interesting to see how Paul signifies or speaks sarcastically about such great thinkers as Aristotle. When Paul uses words like *length* and *breadth* and *height* and *depth* in verse 18, you should know that Paul is making fun of Aristotle. This great philosopher said in his *Metaphysic* that we should trust the senses above all else. In other words, if you can't see and touch and measure a thing, don't depend on it. So Paul suggests, with some sarcasm, that the saints ought to know the measurements of the love of Christ. He is boldly hinting that no yardstick ever measured the most important thing in the world, which is the love of Christ, not science, even though we do need science. In everyday language, the greatest wisdom is spiritual insight, which uses all other wisdom to accomplish the purposes of love.

Motherwit or common sense, the awesome wisdom of unschooled elders.

One example of this wisdom is what we have called motherwit or common sense, the awesome wisdom of unschooled elders. And we have also seen highly educated persons who didn't have common sense. They were tragic failures. Motherwit is very high intelligence, seasoned with love and spiritual insight. Our ancestors had smarts enough not to be crushed by slavery, evidencing very high intelligence. And even the drug dealers and gamblers of our time often show very high intelligence. They ought, however, to put their brains to better purposes.

Years ago I saw a Sidney Poitier movie in which he, a shrewd gambling operator, fell in love with a domestic worker named Ivy, a housemaid for the rich White folks. When he married Ivy and she left her job, the household where she had worked just plain fell apart. Nobody could get along with anybody else, and all sorts of problems arose. It turned out that Ivy had been much more than a maid; she was the resident "shrink" or psychotherapist. Of course, she was paid as a maid, but she should have been getting fifty dollars an hour minimum for therapy. That was what other people with her skills were able to charge.

When I was pastor of a church in Santa Monica, near Hollywood and Beverly Hills, I had members just like Ivy. One of the most popular and gifted actors in Hollywood was married to a woman who could not manage to get through a day unless she had a heavy dose of alcohol or the steadying influence of her "maid" Laura. Weekends were the wife's worst times. When Laura wasn't at church, I could always be sure she was babysitting or counseling the boss's sick wife. Laura, too, was paid as a maid, but she had the skills of a therapist and the love of Christ. You could never pay a woman like her what she was really worth. She had real wisdom seasoned by love.

But somebody may be wondering about school wisdom. "Reverend, are you saying that we don't need anything but motherwit, no book learning?" Well, I'm glad you asked. That's the other kind of gift I promised to discuss. We need to know, also, that we have born in us the brains that we need in school and business. We have gifts in subjects like mathmatics, language, and business. We are comfortable with motherwit, but we need book learning also. Today, you hardly find one without the other, because of so much technology.

First of all, we should know that Blacks in Africa *invented* math as we know it. The numbers we use are called Arabic numerals, because they came from North Africa. But when this numerical system was invented, North Africa was Black. White people in the Roman Empire had been using Roman numerals, with the Xs and Vs and Is. Can you imagine trying to do your income tax with Roman numerals? Thank God for Arabic numerals and the arithmetic and algebra we now have, and thank God for the native ability that Black people still have, to master their ancestors' invention.

Many years ago I lived near an elementary school where they had a White teacher who didn't believe that little African American boys and girls were dumb in math. She acted like she thought they were smart, and she taught math to fifth graders, going all the way to aspects of calculus. These children didn't know either, about how they weren't supposed to be able to do math. So they just followed the teacher and did what she said do. Somebody should have multiplied that teacher by thousands.

The big question now is what happened to all that Black mathmatical genius? Once in a while I hear of it in a Black astronaut, like MacNair, or read a book about a chemist named George Carver, who grew up in the worst of conditions. I wish there were more African Americans working in the sciences, because the best known math minds where I grew up were the operators of the "numbers" racket. They could do more math in their heads than many folks can do with computers.

Some young brother just said in his mind, "If we're all that smart, then why do we flunk math all the time?" Well, it's not that we don't have the brains; it's a matter of *believing* we don't have math skills, and then fulfilling our own prophecies. One name for it is a mental block. A good dose of faith in God and confidence in the brains God gave us would cure this block in a hurry. I have met many Black students in graduate school who dearly loved math and were better in it than in reading or sociology. Most of us would do well in math if we could shake off the mistaken notion that we can't.

Our job now is to break out of this bad habit and get the maximum out of those brains we didn't know we had. One doesn't just ask God for the knowledge and wait for it to fall from heaven. The raw ability has already been given us, but we have to do our part to bring it out and put it to work. We can bring out our latent talents in two easy steps: think and read as hard as we can, and use this growth for the purposes God assigns. After that, we can watch God bless the effort. Let me explain.

We have to think just as far as we can, to "ze edge of ze abyss," and then "ve take ze leap of faith."

Think and read as far as we can. Minds are like muscles; they go flabby if they are not exercised. We can't ask God to improve our minds, when they are already used entirely too little. God will not do for us what we can do for ourselves. I had a teacher named Paul Tillich who once said that we have to think just as far as we can, to "ze edge of ze abyss," and *then* "ve take ze leap of faith." Tremendous insights from the love of Christ come only when we have done all the thinking we could. Then we look up and say, "Now, Lord."

We can say, "Now, Lord," when we have tried as hard as we could and also when we plan to use our brains for God's kingdom purposes. The love of Christ cannot be employed for hateful ends. Let me share a very personal testimony. When I entered college fifty-seven years ago, I was tested like everyone else, and my score was low, well below median. I had a slow, ghetto-level reading rate, and there was no reason to expect me to accomplish very much. I would never have dreamed of writing books or teaching in graduate schools. Yet I now do both, and I have to look back and wonder how I got over, as we say. One thing I know; my work in Black Church Studies did not come from reading other folks' books. Neither did it come from extensive analytical field research. The books and lectures came literally from going as far as I could and then saying, "Now, Lord!" Results and conclusions that could have taken months to develop came in weeks and even days. I tell you, I can never stop praising my Lord and the surpassing wisdom that is poured out for those who love and trust the God of all Truth, and who need the wisdom right now.

The final step in the process is to be alert and carefully watch our Lord at work in these matters. God uses serious thinking and study for *surprising* results, when they are devoted to Kingdom causes. Whatever education you have or don't have, I dare you to get rooted and grounded and come to know the love of Christ, which surpasses "knowledge."

This knowledge was obvious in a minister who was grounded in the love of Christ, and in the widsom that surpasses formal training. The Reverend T. C. Wynn was pastor at Merced, but he was known and respected by pastors of all races all over the San Joaquin Valley. Despite his poor writing and no formal education, they all came to him for counseling.

When he heard that Ella Mitchell was confined with a clot in her lung, he drove down to visit her. In his kind, fatherly way he chatted and diagnosed. Then he said, "Sister Mitchell, let me tell you a little story."

With that he launched a tale about a missionary on a journey through a jungle, where jeeps and horses could not carry him. At the fall of night, he was hardly halfway through the heavy growth. As he sat in utter darkness by a tree, he had thoughts of wild beasts having him for breakfast. In his terror he began to pray. Then a soothing thought came to him. "He that keepeth Israel neither slumbers nor sleeps." Then he said to God, "Well since you ain't going to sleep nohow, ain't no use of both of us staying awake." With that he fell into deep sleep and arose rested the next morning to continue his journey.

Wynn had diagnosed what none of us professionals had seen. My wife was in crisis because she was utterly helpless. No matter how gladly she was served by us, she had a subconscious drive to somehow earn her own care and respect. Yet she could hardly move. The Reverend Wynn's story was relevant to her need. It did not matter that nobody lives in jungles or passes through them on foot. But the point was dead on target.

Sister Mitchell had to give up and let the merciful Good Shepherd and others care for her. She heard the Reverend Wynn's tale quite clearly, and she soon threw off what had been her massive depression. "When things seem utterly helpless, let God take the responsibility."

The best cure in the world was trust, and the Reverend Wynn had the motherwit and inspired storytelling to prescribe the kind of faith-cure needed.

The Reverend Wynn had gnarled hands from picking as much as four-hundred pounds of cotton in a day. He spoke like people speak in the country, and he wrote with awkward letters nearly an inch high. But he was rooted and grounded in the love of Christ, and his "country widsom" surpassed all professional degrees.

Now that folks can go to schools that were denied the Reverend Wynn, we need to read and study all that we can, but we should not forget the love of Christ and that spirit-filled motherwit. We may teach and write all we can, but we want to stay close to Christ and his love, so we can discern in people what no book can teach. We're going to pray and think all we can, but we know that if we ever manage to help the people, it will only be because the love of Christ adds knowledge that passes all understanding.

And we'll always hold up our heads and know that God hands out the ability to think to all races equally.

Over against all the pomp and circumstance of the rich,
Over against all the privations of the poor,
Over against all the sprawling mansions,
Over against all the cotton patch shacks,
Standeth our God, who is no respecter of persons.
I'm so glad Black children still have a chance.
I'm so glad nobody but God can tell what they shall be.
Human beings may discriminate and try to keep us down;
Systems may lock the doors and try to keep us out,
But Christ is eternal, and this world's systems pass away.
The systems have the riches for the time being, only.
But Christ has control of all the wisdom all the time.
    Forever and ever, forever and ever. Hallelujah!

Questions for Discussion

The Cornerstone Conspiracy

1. The word *cornerstone* in the King James Version is the same as a "capstone" or "keystone." It is the head or middle stone at the top of an arch of brick or stone. Take it out, and both sides fall, yet it is odd in shape. Look up Psalm 118:22. What does it mean here in reference to the Jewish minority?
2. How does the metaphor of a rejected stone apply to you as a person?
3. How does the metaphor of a rejected stone apply to African Americans?
4. Have you ever rejected anybody and regretted it? Tell about it.
5. What was Jesus saying about himself with this metaphor?

Wisdom Redefined

1. Discuss the difference between ignorance and illiteracy? Is a person always ignorant if that person cannot read?
2. Describe old saints you've known who were calm under pressure, and very wise. How much formal education did they have?

3. Discuss African Americans you've known at school who were very bright scholars. Were their parents all very bright, with college educations?
4. Do bright and well-educated parents always have children who are good scholars? Why the seeming differences between parents and their children?
5. Have you ever used all the gifts God gave you in your school or other work? What do you suppose would happen if you did? Discuss one gift in particular.

CHAPTER 7

Self-Esteem and
Black Culture

*For every individual his or her own cultural identity is a function of that
of his or her own people.*[1]

nother source of low self-esteem among African Americans is the notion that our culture is inferior. Even well
meaning writers allege that we were "stripped" of all
culture during the horrors of the Middle Passage, cross-
ing the Atlantic. Nothing could be further from the truth. White
people didn't pass laws against drumming until they were already
sure that this innocent African rhythm was also a sophisticated,
three-tone code for telegraphy. Much of the best medicine in the
early colonies was African and homeopathic. Practice on masters
was forbidden by law only after the mean ones were found to have
unusually poor prognoses. Slaves also kept their original African
worship and ethical value systems, which are a part of African
American survival and great strength even today.

There are African cultural survivals in both church and street
culture. A cultural nostalgia for the extended family society is
evident today when street people in the ghetto still call one
another brother and sister. And abandoned children may still be
taken in by the few who can't resist the compassion in their bones.
It was just such compassion that forced the highly placed Ebed-
melech to stop and heed the cry of Jeremiah in the cistern. It drove

him to risk his high position and confront the king also. A materialistic culture may see such compassion as weakness, but it is strength.

This is the kind of weakness God uses to confound the strong and sustain a people in oppression. We are forced to become competent in not one but two cultures, and this is a major strength. Bicultural competence distinguished the apostle Paul, as well as his protegé, Timothy.

Buppies in the Palace

EMIL THOMAS

But Ebed-Melech, a Cushite, an official in the royal palace, heard that they had put Jeremiah into the cistern.

(JEREMIAH 38:7*a* NIV)
JEREMIAH 38:5-13, 39:15-18

You've heard of the term *Buppies*, haven't you? In the 1960s we had the Hippies and the Yippies. The Hippies were a counter-culture community that advocated an alternative life-style. The Yippies were not only culturally nonconforming, they were also politically active in their stance against the Vietnam War and other issues. Well, Hippies and Yippies have stepped aside and the Yuppies and Buppies have stepped forward. The word *Yuppie* is derived from the letters Y, U, and P, which stand for "Young, Upwardly Mobile Professional." *Buppie* is similar—it just means "Black Upwardly Mobile Professional." Yuppies and Buppies have already made an impact on American society.

Ever since I've been a preacher I've been a people-watcher. I've become somewhat of a specialist as a Buppie-Watcher. These days, Buppies seem to be everywhere. Buppies at the Mall, Buppies downtown, Buppies at the university, Buppies at the theater, Buppies in BMWs. It's an "Old MacDonald" situation: here a Buppie, there a Buppie, everywhere a Buppie Buppie!

Now don't get me wrong; I am not using the term in a derisive manner. I like Buppies. I can relate to Buppies. I think that somewhere in my heart of hearts I want to fellowship with the Buppie society. Buppies are invited to attend and join our churches just like all of God's children. And since I have always appreciated W. E. B Dubois' vision of the "Talented Tenth," I continue to nourish hopes and dreams that God will use Buppies to uplift all African Americans.

But my hopes and dreams are tempered by fears of what might happen to Buppies when they reach the palace. As high as we may rise in the corporate palaces of the business world, I hope that we will never forget that there is somebody in the dungeon.

Ebed-melech was a Buppie in the Palace. He was a highly trained, highly competent, trusted, and respected member of the administrative staff of King Zedekiah of Judah. I know that he was super-talented, because he was a foreigner, an African from the glorious land of Ethiopia. And whenever a Black person gets a position in a foreign land, he or she is at least twice as competent as their competitors. From Barbara Jordan to Douglas Wilder, from Carol Mosely-Braun to Colin Powell—African Americans have had to be overachievers in their fields to gain the respect that comes more easily to a colleague from the dominant society.

The word *eunuch* that is attached to Ebed-melech is a chilling reminder that for Black males, sometimes the cost of success is emasculation. But biblical commentators and scholars note that this word is most often a description of high rank rather than of neutered masculinity.

Ebed-melech had everything that a man could desire in his day or our day: wealth, honor, position, power, and the run of the palace. But one day something disturbing happened. While strolling past the dungeon of Malchiah the son of Hammelech, he heard sounds that interrupted his peace of mind. Tortured groans and agonizing moans were emanating from the dungeon. Removing the cover from this underground cistern, his eyes were shocked at what they beheld. Jeremiah, the weeping prophet, was languishing in the bowels of the dungeon. His sunken eyes and emaciated arms revealed that he was dying of starvation. The trickle of sunlight that crept in betrayed that his legs and hips were gradually sinking in the mud, muck, and mire at the bottom of this old well. A conversation with the incarcerated preacher revealed that he was there because he dared to proclaim what "thus said the Lord." Ebed-melech recovered the dungeon and began a painful promenade back to the palace. The dungeon had placed him in a dilemma. Should he risk his rank to rescue this preacher? Should he jeopardize his job to emancipate this prophet? "Oh, if only I had gone another way," he lamented. The terrible tension almost tore him in two. He tried to put it out of his mind, but his conscience wouldn't let him.

On one hand, there was Zedekiah—on the other hand, there was Jeremiah;

On one hand, there was the palace—on the other hand, there was the dungeon;

On one hand, there was power—on the other hand, there was pain;

On one hand, there was success—on the other hand, there was suffering;

On one hand, there was life—on the other hand, there was death.

Ebed-melechs have not vanished from the earth. There are Ebed-melechs living in America, working in the industrial and educational palaces of this nation, and walking the streets of cities all across this country. They are highly trained, highly competent, supertalented African Americans in the flower of success. But every now and then, they pass by the dungeon. It may be on a suburban street where a homeless person with a shopping cart cries from a dungeon for some change to get food to eat. It may be at the grocery store when you look into the eyes of an older person and see instead of joy a dungeon of loneliness and abandonment. It may be in the ghetto where a young boy who looks like you did when you were a teenager comes to your car window and turns your BMW into a dungeon by offering you some crack cocaine. If you're anything like Ebed-melech, you can't be contented. Though you try to put it out of your mind, it keeps coming back. You know that dungeons may be dark, but they are not without hope. Dungeons may echo with the negative emotions of degradation and despair, but you know that there is a way out. If God can lift you above the odds, then that same God can lift another out of his or her dungeon.

Ebed-melech made up his mind. Ebed-melech left the royal halls of the palace with fire in his eyes, looking for King Zedekiah. He was not halting, hesitating, or half-stepping either. His head held high, he was moving with resolve, and I can almost hear him singing a tune to himself:

> If I can help somebody as I pass along, . . .
> Then my living shall not be in vain.[2]

Ebed-melech was a sixth-century Buppie, but I told you that I like Buppies. I believe that Buppies have some resources that some Yuppies may not have. But the resources of the Buppies don't come from their secular success in the palace, but from the old-time religion, that down-home Black culture that got them to the palace. If you don't believe me, just look at the resources that Ebed-melech used to turn a dungeon dilemma into deliverance!

Toughness

I know that Ebed-melech was not a wimp, a chump, or a pushover. His response to Jeremiah's imprisonment is graphic evidence that this Buppie was *tough*. The scene shifts to the Gate of Benjamin where King Zedekiah is sitting. This was much like a public court in which the king was making legal decisions and judging cases in the land. Ebed-melech was so bold, so assertive, and so confrontational that he interrupted the proceedings with an embarrassing announcement: "my lord the king, these men have done evil in all that they have done to Jeremiah the prophet, whom they have cast into the dungeon; and he is likely to die from hunger in the place where he is: for there is no more bread in the city" (Jer. 38:9). Zedekiah was on the spot. He knew that he was the one who gave the orders to cast Jeremiah into the dungeon, but now he had to release him, or his public image would be damaged.

Ebed-melech risks position, life and limb in challenging the king. His toughness brought deliverance to the dungeon.

There is a great temptation for modern-day Buppies to be taken by the lure of the palace, intoxicated by the taste of power, and nullified by cultural assimilation. Those in the palace would have you think that you are there out of the goodness of their hearts. They want you to believe that because of affirmative action, you are a token representative—an ethnic curio on their shelf only there to meet statistical requirements. But we know that we have not come this far on the goodness of men, but by the grace of God. "We've come this far by faith, leaning on the Lord." God has blessed us, and God has brought us. And God didn't bring us up the rough side of the mountain so we could master the art of bowing, scraping, kowtowing, head-scratching, and genuflecting. God brought us to "let our lights so shine before people that they may see our good works and glorify our Father who is in heaven." We cannot sing "Stand Up, Stand Up for Jesus" as long as we are scared of another individual. The toughness that was developed on the journey was a gift of grace to make us strong in the hour of testing.

Ebed-melech was moved to revulsion by the injustice and inhumanity experienced by a man of God. Never mind that he was a dignitary of the royal court. He could not look down his nose at the plight of the preacher. He didn't learn that at the university! Traditional Black culture that refuses to split the sacred from the secular taught him to reverence the prophet!

This is a way that you can tell if you have really made it or not. Can you convert your influence in the palace to be used for the good of someone in need? Can you confront the "king" in order to make a change in world affairs? Are you tough enough to challenge your boss, your teacher, or your professor on issues of injustice and inhumanity? Martin Luther King, Jr., said that our world is in trouble, not so much because of the vitriolic pronouncements of bad people, but because of the appalling silence of good people. When there is inhumanity to God's children, you ought to say something! Ebed-melech was tough enough to challenge the king on a matter of injustice and human rights, even to help an old preacher in a well!

Togetherness

This Buppie was not a Lone Ranger type of personality. Ebed-melech did not have a messiah-complex; believing that he was going to solve all of the problems of the world by himself. Though he was a self-starter and was not afraid to be an initiator, he knew that he could accomplish a lot more with help. When King Zedekiah ordered a palace guard and an entourage to accompany him, he did not foolishly reject the offer. He knew the advantage and protective power of *togetherness.*

Why is it that some Buppies try to go it alone? Why is it that once they hit it big they don't want to fellowship or associate with anybody anymore? Why is it that some individuals believe that once they have a few letters after their names they don't need any advice? Why is it that once people move into the neighborhood of the palace they don't like to drive by the dungeon where they came from anymore? It is at least partly because some Buppies have adopted the Western emphasis on individual success and have forgotten the Black cultural emphasis on communal survival.

It is a dangerous thing to isolate oneself from others. My mother once said, "Don't forget the bridge that crossed you over—you may have to cross it again some day. Don't forget the house you used to live in, somebody's living there now. The same people you pass on the way up, you will pass on the way down."

Ebed-melech knew that there is both power and protection in numbers. It would be hard for him to lift Jeremiah from the dungeon by himself, but thirty men could marshal more power. If we as a people would come together, we could save our families, save our colleges, and pull our people out of the dungeon. He also knew that when you try to lift somebody up, somebody will try to tear you down. The same people who wanted Jeremiah imprisoned were probably lurking in the shadows, waiting for Ebed-melech to try to pull something like this. Like crabs in the proverbial bucket, there are always some people who would rather pull people down than lift them up. With this protecting group of men, together, they would have both the power and protection to lift the suffering prophet from the dungeon and his sure demise.

Tenderness

But look! Not only does Ebed-melech possess toughness and togetherness, he also has *tenderness!* Look at the compassion in his ministry of emancipation and liberation. He takes this detachment of thirty men to a storehouse of rotten rags and cast-off garments. Befuddled and bewildered, they follow him to the dungeon to see what will occur. What is this Black man doing with all of these rags? Has he gone mad? When they arrive, they see Ebed-melech's tenderness unfold. Jeremiah, wasting away in the cold and damp dungeon, is nothing but skin and bones. His muscles are so emaciated that if they tried to pull him from the muddy bog at the bottom of the cistern, they may cut his arms or make the enterprise wholly impossible. The rags are there to provide a benevolent cushion in consideration of the old prophet's plight.

Sometimes in trying to help someone, we can do more harm than good. Sometimes the manner in which we lift someone may damage them permanently. It is so easy to forget that no matter how low someone is on the social ladder, they deserve consideration. They deserve respect. They deserve human dignity. Have you ever seen someone condescendingly and indiscreetly ask a suffering person what they need? And then after the person, in their humble pride, says that they don't need anything, they act like they're offended, saying, "I tried to help them, child, but he didn't want it." That is not considerate of the fact that all people, even those who are homeless and drug-addicted, have a sense of dignity. Emancipation and consideration go together. Liberation and compassion go together. Rescue, respect, and dignity all are woven together in the tapestry of tenderness. Ebed-melech had not forgotten how to be tender. Thus, Ebed-melech, the Ethiopian emancipator, wrought Jeremiah's deliverance from the dungeon.

Trust

After the episode, Jeremiah eventually went to the home of Gedaliah, who would become the governor of Judea, and Ebed-melech went back to the palace. But before Jeremiah left the confines of the court of the prison, he mused and meditated on the meaning of what had transpired. It was one of the strangest things he had ever experienced. Here he had been in a dungeon. He was placed there by his own people for saying "What thus said the Lord."

Deliverance often comes from the most unexpected places. This time it came not from a friend, but from a foreigner; not from a Semite, but from a Hamite; not from an Asiatic, but from an African. I believe that it was in his time of reflection that God gave him insight into this Buppie's intercession and intervention. The Lord gave Jeremiah another word, another sermon—this time not to his own Jewish people, but for this African. "Go and speak to Ebed-melech the Ethiopian. . . . I will [destroy this city]. But I will deliver thee in that day, saith the LORD. . . . I will surely deliver thee, and thou shall not fall by the sword, but thy life shall be a [prize] unto thee: because thou hast put thy trust in me, saith the LORD" (Jer. 39:16-18).

The greatest resource of this Buppie named Ebed-melech was not his toughness, nor his togetherness, nor his tenderness, but his *trust* in the Lord! Whenever you trust in the Lord, you are leaning on someone who has more clout than the king! When you trust in the Lord you are depending on someone who has more power than you can put in a palace! And there is a special blessing for Buppies like Ebed-melech—if you trust in God, and help someone else out of their dungeon, the Lord will be there to deliver you from *your* dungeon! In the New Testament, Jesus says it this way: "Anyone who receives a prophet because he is a prophet will receive a prophet's reward. . . . And if anyone gives a cup of cold water to one of these . . . , he will certainly not lose his reward" (Matt. 10:41, 42 NIV).

The word *Ebed-melech* means "servant of the king." Zedekiah probably thought he was a great candidate for a palace position because anyone who is named "servant of the king" would be psychologically conditioned to be loyal to a king. But what Zedekiah didn't know was that Ebed-melech was serving a King who was higher than Zedekiah! He was trusting a King that ruled the world and "super-ruled" the universe! Ebed-melech was not leaning on Zedekiah! Ebed-melech was not depending on Zedekiah! Ebed-melech was not leaning on Zedekiah's position! Ebed-melech was not depending on Zedekiah's palace! Ebed-melech was a servant of the King of kings and the Lord of lords!

Ebed-melech is a model for all modern-day Buppies! Though he knew how to make a *living,* he never forgot how to make a *leaning!* I thank God that from the earliest point of my existence, I was exposed to a lot of Ebed-Melechs. I saw them as I grew up in the Mt. Olive Baptist Church of Flint, Michigan. They knew *who* they were, and they also knew *whose* they were! They knew where they had come from, and they also knew where they were going! They could teach you how to make a *living,* but they could also testify about how they made their *leaning!* Some of them even had a *leaning* song! It went something like this:

> I've learned how to lean and depend on Jesus!
> I've learned how to lean and depend on Jesus!
> I've learned how to lean and depend on Jesus;
> I found out, if I trust him he will provide![3]

Epistle to the Young, Gifted, and Black

HENRY H. MITCHELL

Therefore, I remind you to stir up the gift of God that is in you.

II TIMOTHY 1:6 (AP)

Years ago, a very popular singer named Nina Simone hit the charts with a song about Black self-esteem: "To Be Young, Gifted, and Black." It celebrated a set of talents that all too many Black youths seemed not even to know they had. In today's world, with its horrible statistics about urban ghettos, there are even *more* youths who ought to be awakened to their real potential. The big question is simply, How on earth do you convince young people that their greatest hope, in this seemingly hopeless situation, is in their own God-given gifts?

Paul's letter to this young man named Timothy had the same goal in mind, to help him become aware of his potential—to see for himself just how smart he was. Paul had watched Timothy as he grew up among an oppressed racial and religious minority called Jewish Christians. Paul had come to admire Tim's grandma, Lois, and his mother, Eunice, so much that he praised them higher than anybody else in his letters. Paul really needed people like this.

"Stir up the gift of God in you."

Paul encountered a small, young movement, which had a great shortage of leadership. There weren't enough seasoned and gifted believers to head up these young churches he was starting. Paul saw in this young Timothy the very potential he needed so badly. So he wrote him to say that he knew he was capable and called, and to suggest that he accept official ordination. The crux of the letter is summed up in eight words, all having only one syllable: *"Stir up the gift of God in you."* Now, of course, we all wonder what kind of gifts this youth—this kid—could have had for dealing with slightly shaky Christians like the Thessalonians, to say nothing of the Corinthians. We look on the lines and between the lines of the text. And we examine some of Paul's other letters and the Acts of the Apostles to find the answers.

No doubt Timothy was bright. Paul, who was a very intelligent man himself, was quite impressed with Timothy's intellectual gifts. We don't know exactly *how* he knew this, but the very assignments he gave Timothy suggest that he must have been a very astute person. One doesn't tell young persons to let nobody despise their youth, unless those youths have the brains to make up for their lack

123

of experience. Paul went so far as to challenge Tim to be a model and a *teacher* of the Word (I Tim. 4:12-13). Timothy's sharp and agile mind, stimulated by much time under Paul, gave him enough of an edge that Timothy could teach older saints with no hesitation.

Tim's natural, God-given intelligence was enhanced by another gift that Paul knew very well. Both Paul and Tim could deal with not one but *two* cultures. Tim's father was Greek and his home folks spoke Greek. His whole hometown of Lystra spoke and thought Greek. They were a part of the culture and civilization that flowed up from Africa and made Greece great. As much as any other gifted kid who grew up in Lystra, Tim could deal with Greek language and learning. He was completely at ease preaching in Greek.

At the same time he was deep into the soulful culture of his Jewish mother and grandma. He knew the language of the kinfolks who shared the lot of Jews in the Diaspora, the Jews driven out of their homeland. He was at ease with the "down-home" brothers and sisters of the hood. He was what they call bicultural. He was like one of us who can deal with the Black folks *and* the White folks also. Like his mentor, Paul, he could be many things to many people.

And this leads to the third great gift Tim had, the gift of deep and strong religious roots. When Paul remembered the sincere faith of Lois and Eunice, he had no doubt that Tim had been deeply influenced by this same powerful belief system.

Just how deep their faith had become is seen not only in the admiration Paul had for them, but in a scan of their family history. Up to the point where he was named Timothy, this family had been trying to get *away* from their Jewish roots. Timothy was a *Greek* name, not a David or a Jacob. Lois and Eunice also had Greek names, which suggests that they were trying to disappear among the fair-skinned majority—to help people forget that they were Jews. Eunice married a Greek. Tim was not even circumcised as a Jew until Paul had it done, so Tim could minister to the Jewish Christians at Corinth. In a word, Lois and family must have had a great group conversion for them to stop trying to pass for Greeks and go all the way with Jesus. And they did go all the way, or Paul would never have said what he said. Nor would he have been so certain of Timothy's deep religious roots and upbringing.

These roots were not only a great gift or head start for Tim's calling as an apostle; these religious roots would have been a tremendous advantage for him or anybody else. The strength of character and the endurance of people with religion this deep will help one go to the top in *any* field. So the gifts Paul wanted Tim to stir up were a powerful advantage, empowering Timothy to work among a people who were racially and religiously oppressed.

The important thing is to know that any one of us will likely have most if not actually all of these easily overlooked gifts. And so we need to *stir them up*, as one stirs up the embers of a fire almost gone out, with much wood still left.

Dear Young, Gifted, and Black:

What's goin' down? I know you don't expect a seventy-five-year-old man to talk all that talk, but we need to think together right now, to see if we can stop all this shootin' and dyin' and, most of all, get to where we can have some hope and some peace and power. Does that get to you? And since nobody else seems to be interested enough or capable enough to deal with it, we have to get down and deal with it ourselves. There's nobody else to save us.

Now the first thing we need to face up to is the fact that we may think we're helpless, but we aren't. There are a lot of people telling us we're dumb, for instance, but we have as many brains as anybody. Just 'cause we who live in the ghetto don't have a lot of money, that doesn't mean we're automatically dumb.

If you think we're dumb, deal with the brothers selling dope and running numbers and try to cheat them. Those dudes got computers in their heads, and they make fewer mistakes than the bank does. With the brains they have and some education, they could deal on Wall Street as well as anyone. The problem is that certain folks and conditions have conspired to make them think they're dumb, so they drop out of school and try to take short cuts to long cars and fat wallets. But that only works for a little while, and then eventually they end up in jail, or dead.

I know we got all kinds of brains and talents, because I've seen it in all sorts of places. And you have too. We know how to hustle wherever the system lets us in. In sports we don't just throw or shoot balls; we make the boss pay us millions. In showbiz we are funnier than anybody else. We get over no matter how much or how little artistic talent we may have. It takes real brains to do the things we do so well.

In a swanky hotel in Stockholm, Sweden, there was this great big crowd in the lobby, standing around a piano. The voice we heard singing was pretty good, but nothing to write home about. It was a light baritone, with a mostly faked, by-ear piano accompaniment. When we finally wormed our way up to where we could see, guess what! This was a sister from home, singin' and playin' at the same time. That crowd was eatin' it up! She didn't have a golden voice, but she was a smart entertainer. I tell you God gave all of us some talent, and it will get us over somewhere! My point is that Africans invented math and medicine, and carved beautiful granite columns long before the Greeks. We, too, have gifts born in us, because God fixed it that way. Every race has some very smart people, and that includes us.

Then we have another type of gift; we can be like Paul and Timothy and deal with more than one culture. We have been an oppressed minority, so we had no choice but to learn ours and theirs. Yet every culture we have adds to our wisdom and our ability to deal. It helps to be forced to know more.

In addition to Black music and sports and cooking, we have some great habits or traditions, and often it is something we are a little ashamed of. Like, look at a Black funeral in the ghetto, and a White funeral in the suburbs. White Protestants have a quiet, fifteen-minute memorial service. We say they are dignified, and we think we ought to stop having long funerals and so much emotion. Well let me tell you, we cry and go back to work. Other folks, who didn't let themselves do their grief work, go home and die holding it in, or letting it out when they are all alone. Any psychiatrist will tell you, if the grief is real and sincere, Black cultural systems for letting it out are better every time.

And here's another part of our culture that's really stupid, which means cool. We may be poor as anything, but maybe except in the big cities, we tend to share, and lots of people know it. Even in the cities, social workers go crazy trying to understand how many extended family members are helped by one welfare check. One person has a check today, and another has some sort of check next week. Even now, one can find whole neighborhoods here and there that are just like families, and everybody helps to raise everybody else's kids. I could go on and on naming Black culture characteristics that make me very proud and happy to be who I am. When you look at the fact that we have all this powerful Black tradition and also know something about how to deal with the White majority's ways, you have to know that we are specially blessed. We are as gifted as anybody else, and we can deal in two cultures.

But there is one more gift that I think is more important than either of the other two; it is our African American Christian religion. Now I know you are wondering what earthly good that could possibly be. You may even have heard somebody sing, "Gimme that ole time religion, it's good enough for me." And you may have wondered, "Good for what?"

Well, in the first place, it's good for keeping us alive and still in our right minds. If our slave ancestors had not had a hope in Jesus, they would have had no hope at all, and they would have gone crazy or committed suicide. When you see Black youths doing suicide today, it's because they've lost that hope. But among most of us even now, we praise God more and self-destruct less than the most wealthy and comfortable of our oppressors. We still can't make it through this troublesome world without the same faith that kept our ancestors' heads up and feet running.

Then there's the feeling part of our religion. Many young people get ashamed of our ways of worship; they think it's a sign of ignorance. Many others like the soulful warmth of our tradition. Of course, fake warmth and put-on shouting is dead wrong. But sincere expression of deep feeling not only praises God; it heals and strengthens the person of faith. It is most important that in a hostile world, we have had a place where we could be and act just who we were. We can let it all hang out and know that God and the sisters and brothers understood and are giving support. Many a sister or brother has been able to make it all week because of the healing and strength they gained from our soulful Sunday worship.

The truth is that instead of trying to be like the majority, we can do the opposite and let folks see just how much our kind of faith means to us and could mean to them. We have seen this sort of a move already in show business. Everybody knows that the best of performers, from Elvis Presley on down, got their style and inspiration from African Americans like Bo Diddley and many others. They get more money for our songs than we do, but at least it's quite clear that they recognize our genuine soul culture as the most desirable music there is. And what we can say about the U.S.A. can be said about nearly anywhere else in the world. It's just too bad that our spirituals, our gospels, and our preaching have not been as widely shared as our entertainment music. Imagine what the world would be like if spirituals were as widely influential as the blues and jazz coming originally out of our spiritual music.

We've already had a taste of how our stuff can be effective. The most important single speech made in America since Lincoln's Gettysburg Address is undoubtedly the "I Have Dream" sermon of Martin Luther King, Jr., made at the Lincoln Monument in Washington, D.C., in 1963. It was a classic example of all three of the kinds of gifts Timothy had and we have. Martin King was born sharp; he came here with the gift of native intelligence from God. He was a scholar in White culture, all the way to a Ph.D.; but he could rap to his sisters and brothers in their language also. He was also bicultural. And the third gift, his religious heritage from his grandparents and his parents, was awesome. God used all three gifts to sway not only the 300,000 people present there in Washington; it was a speech heard round the world, by television and radio. And that speech changed, and continues to change, the world.

If you are ever tempted to think you're a nobody, with no talents and no way to make anything happen for yourself or your people, just think of this brother named Martin, who literally changed the world. America will never again return to raw, legalized discrimination. East Germans—reading Martin's writings, singing the movement's songs, and using the strategies Martin designed—tore down the Berlin wall. Not a shot was fired, not a drop of blood shed, but Berlin will never again be the same.

Russia, the country we feared so much that we wasted billions in defense, had a revolution. The yoke of dictatorial Communism was thrown off. To the surprise of all, the people are free and, again, they sing Martin's songs and try to use the nonviolent methods he so seriously taught.

Word up, young sisters and brothers! You will never know how many gifts you have and how much you can change the world until you try. When I remember the sincere faith that was in your enslaved great grandparents, I am persuaded that it is in you also. I challenge you to stir up the gifts of God that are in you.

You are young and strong, with enough time to get the job done. Oh, thank God for being young and full of energy!

You are gifted with amazing brains, as well as showbiz and sports. Oh, thank God for all this talent we've been overlooking!

You are Black, African American, with the ability to make it in more than one world, and with roots in good religion. Oh, thank God for all this Blackness gives to us!

God has not given us the spirit of fear, but of power, and of love, and of self-control. So stir up the gift!

I mean, let's get busy; we're young, gifted, and Black!

Let's get busy; we are not afraid, and we're young, gifted, and Black!

Let's get busy; we have unused power and mighty love, and we're young, gifted, and Black!

Let's get busy; we are cool and self-controlled, and we are young, gifted, and Black!

It's time to get busy and take control of our own destiny.

I can see the day when just as our music is heard everywhere, our wisdom and love will be talked about around the world.

Just as our athletes are celebrated everywhere, our Dr. Kings and our Mary Bethunes, our Barbara Jordans and our Thurgood Marshalls will be praised around the world for having helped to bring justice and to save our world from cruelty and greed.

I thank God for all of you, with all these gifts! My hopes are high because of you and your gifts. Now stir them up, and let's get busy!

Your older brother in Christ,
Henry Mitchell

Questions for Discussion

Buppies in the Palace

1. Do you consider yourself or your family to be Buppies? Do you have a general impression of Buppies? What is it?
2. Some Buppies have been known to sever all extended family and ghetto community ties. What are the advantages of such escape?

3. Ebed-melech found it impossible to forget what he heard and saw in the cistern. Are all African peoples that compassionate?

4. What did Ebed-melech gain by his response of compassion, and what did he lose by confronting the king?

5. Note Ebed-melech's strategy for lifting Jeremiah out of the cistern. What can be learned from the way he went about it? What resources do we have for helping one another today?

Epistle to the Young, Gifted, and Black

1. What is your opinion of Lois and Eunice's original decision to "pass," with Greek names, culture, and religion? Do you sympathize?

2. Can you imagine how they came to such a complete reversal that their sincere faith gets the highest praise Paul ever gave? What would it have taken to break out of their false security?

3. Give your own appraisal of Timothy's gifts that Paul said could be an example to older folks and that he told him to stir up.

4. What are the advantages of fleeing to where you are comfortable, but cut off from your religious roots?

5. Fully recognizing the problems of oppression, compare the results of self-pity with counting your God-given resources.

CHAPTER 8

Self-Esteem
and Oppressed Existence

The purpose of evil was to survive it and they determined (without ever knowing they had made up their minds to do it) to survive floods, white people, tuberculosis, famine, and ignorance.[1]

nother main source of low self-esteem among African Americans is hard times, or poverty and oppression. Younger sufferers are plagued by the subtle suspicion that their just and provident God has abandoned them and even, at times, that they deserve it. One has to ponder how their enslaved ancestors endured far harder circumstances, and yet had so much more calmness and self-esteem.

One obvious reason for this is higher expectations among the young. Constantly exposed to the more comfortable living standards of others, their sense of impoverishment is huge. But the answer to this disappointment is certainly not to be found in turning the clock back and lowering expectations. The lasting answers are, first, to work and cry for justice until it happens. For supposedly powerless people, texts like Luke 18:2-8 are good prescriptions for frustration and low self-image. One feels much better about oneself when one is engaged in a demanding struggle, which gives meaning to life, both through the action itself and through the successes achieved from time to time.

The slave ancestors had another basis for calm: a special inner peace, born of a profound conviction that their self-worth had been well established already and was guaranteed by the Ruler of the Universe. This was not mystical, quiescent acceptance of less than their due. Rather, it was their way of depending on God to do what they could not do, *after* having done their best in the struggle for justice. Their trust included the certainty that divine justice would not only properly reward their own struggles and their monumental commitment to love even their enemies, it would also punish the cruelties heaped on them. This punishment (due to the Law of Identical Harvest) was God's way of certifying the intrinsic and inviolable worth of the oppressed in the scheme of Creation.

The Cry for Justice

EMIL THOMAS

He said: "In a certain town there was a judge who neither feared God nor cared about men. And there was a widow in that town who kept coming to him with the plea, 'Grant me justice against my adversary.' "

(LUKE 18:2-3 NIV)
LUKE 18:2-8

(Preached the Sunday following the 1992 Los Angeles Uprising)

The times in which we live are not only trying times but crying times. Who can be unmoved by the chorus of cries that reverberate through the streets of our society? We all understand that when basic human needs go unmet, cries will be heard. Some today are crying for food; for though people cannot live by bread *alone*, people must live by bread *at least*. Others are crying for community, camaraderie, and companionship; for it is not good for people to be alone. Many are crying for shelter; for, like the Son of Man, they see foxes with holes and birds with nests, but they have nowhere to lay their heads. We are haunted by the echoes of myriad cries for employment, health care, and peace on our streets. And yet undergirding all of these cries is the cry for justice.

America is plagued by an epidemic of problems. "Isms" and schisms threaten to rip the very fabric of our culture. We are plagued by the problem of racism, as people continue to judge others on the specificities of their identity rather than the depth of their character. We are plagued by the problem of sexism, as we overlook a person's genius because of her or his gender. We are plagued by problems of classism, as the gap grows between the haves and the have-nots. *Laissez-faire capitalism*, New World Order militarism, modern paganism, and a creeping underground *Nazism* and fascism are all "isms" that bring schisms to our nation.

This plague of problems has provided a platform for our cries for justice. Isn't that what most people want? An even playing field? A fair chance? An equal opportunity? An opportunity to be judged by their character, capabilities, and conduct? Yet I am convinced that in the midst of these problems, we still have the power of God's promises. And God has promised that justice shall roll down as water and righteousness as a mighty stream.

Today God's power and promise can be seen in a parable. In Luke 18, Jesus tells a story of a woman who cried out for justice. We do not learn the details of what had happened, but somehow, this woman was denied justice. She was a widow—was her husband killed? Had her son been brutalized or her daughter assaulted? Had her job been unfairly snatched from her? The details we will never know, but what we do know is that she cried for justice, and in her story is God's powerful promise for our problems.

Notice first this woman's problem—a corrupt court. If you want a good definition of a corrupt court, you'll find it in Jesus' words: "In a certain city, there was a judge who neither feared God, nor cared about people." That's a classic definition of a corrupt court! On one hand there is no fear of God; on the other hand there is no concern for humanity. I submit that whenever you have a court that neither reveres providence nor respects people, you've got a corrupt court!

Though I'm sure there'll be no shouting when I say it, when we look at today's American legal system, we are looking at a corrupt court! I believe that we are losing our fear of God in our legal system. When a court can boldly and blatantly deny justice in full view of God and the whole world, there is no fear of God! When convictions of prominent military leaders get them slaps on their wrists and yet a conviction of James Brown gets him slapped in jail, there is no fear of God! When a poor man goes to prison for murder, yet a rich man is not convicted because of "temporary insanity," there is no fear of God! When the measure of justice you receive is based on the color of your skin or the size of your wallet, there is no fear of God! God does not judge on the basis of color, for the Scriptures declare, "God is no respecter of persons." God does not judge on the basis of cash, because God already owns everything! God judges on the standards of righteousness, the standards that have been revealed to humanity in the Bible.

Why don't our courts fear God? It may be because our leaders often don't care about people. We have now come through more than a decade of governmental policies that gave a ride to the rich on the backs of the poor. That tells me that they don't care about people. Though news broadcasts are decrying the looting of stores in Los Angeles and other cities, no one is decrying the systematic looting that has been taking place for twelve years. That tells me that they don't care about people. The corporations have already looted the inner city of jobs and have shipped them to Mexico, Korea, China, and other countries. The government has looted the schools of money and given massive increases to the military, choosing to buy bullets and bombs instead of blackboards and books. That tells me that they don't care about people.

My father only completed the third grade. Though he had little education, he had revelation. Though his eyesight was weak, his insight was strong. Though he had no degree in his house, he could read the handwriting on the wall. After Mussolini had invaded Ethiopia and World War II had begun, Dad was inspired to enlist for the army and saw time fighting in Italy in the 92nd Infantry, the famous "Buffalo Soldiers." After he died in 1984, I went through his papers and found numerous letters that he had written to the government in order to receive his veteran's benefits. His request was repeatedly denied. About the only thing that he received for fighting in that war was a flag on his coffin. I tell you, our government ought to care more for people!

It is to have eyes that cannot see because they are clouded with the cataracts of cruelty.

Now it is bad enough when you don't fear God. And it is bad as well when you don't care about people. But when you neither fear God nor care about people, you are dangerously insensitive! As a matter of fact, the two are tied together—those who fear God will care about people, and those who altruistically care about people are most open to God. Neither to revere God nor respect people is to be spiritually blind, morally deaf, and emotionally cold. It is to have eyes that cannot see because they are clouded with the cataracts of cruelty. It is to have ears that cannot hear because they are clogged and cluttered with the wax of wickedness. It is to have a heart that has grown fat with the cholesterol of selfishness.

A jury in Simi Valley returned a verdict that was blind, deaf, and dumb. They saw the same videotape that I saw: the most barbaric, brutal beating of a Black man that I have ever witnessed in my life, the most appalling and atrocious act that I have ever seen roll across my television screen. And yet one of the jurors had the gall to say something like: "Well, he wasn't beaten that badly." Yet if I were to go out in the street and beat a dog as Rodney King was beaten, I could be convicted of cruelty to animals! And on top of that, they acquitted the policemen of this crime. That indeed was a corrupt court!

The judge in Jesus' story was insensitive to the woman. He declined to give her justice. But thank God there is more in this passage than a corrupt court.

Note also the power of a consistent cry. Jesus tells us that the woman did not accept the verdict of the court. She went to the judge and cried out to him, and kept coming to him with the plea, "Grant me justice against my adversary."

In first-century Palestine, a widow was perhaps the weakest person in the social order. She was obviously worried, because injustice causes a most profound concern. She was probably weary, because she "kept coming to him" with her plea. But although she was weak, she was not too weak to cry. Although she was worried, she was not too worried to cry. Although she may have been weary, she was not too weary to cry. You see, I don't care how weak, worried, or weary you may be, if you are right, there is always power enough to cry!

There was *continuity* in her cry. Jesus said, "She *kept on* crying." In my mind's eye I can see her continually crying. When the judge got to work in the morning, she was outside of the courthouse crying for justice. When he was leaving for lunch, she was there crying for justice. All day during the proceedings, they could hear her outside crying for justice. When he walked out of the door to go home at 5:00, she was there crying for justice. When he sat down for dinner at night and turned on the evening news, he saw her on television crying for justice. It may have been that even after he went to sleep at night she showed up in his dreams with her haunting cry for justice! I tell you, there was continuity in her cry!

Do you know what has happened to us as Black people? As soon as we got a degree on the wall, a car in the garage, a television in the living room and a microwave in the kitchen, we forgot how to cry! We thought that just because we were admitted to their schools that we didn't need to cry. We thought that just because we moved into their suburbs that we didn't need to cry. We thought that just because we got an executive position in the corporate world that we didn't need to cry. We thought that our integration, assimilation, and acculturation had eliminated our need to cry for justice. But don't ever forget where you have come from, because someone may try to send you back one day!

She did not compromise her cry with corrupt conduct.

I don't care how far you think that you have risen in this society, as long as you are Black, you have not risen too high to stop crying for justice. If you don't believe me, you just get caught on the wrong side of town at the wrong time of night, and make the wrong move when the police ask you to step out of your car. Your name may well replace Rodney King's name in the national consciousness!

There was also *consecration* in this widow's cry. There is no record here that she burned down the judge's house. There is no record that she looted goods from the judge's home. There is no record that she pulled the judge out of his car and beat him within an inch of his life. Her cry was a consecrated cry. She knew that in order to demand justice, she must demonstrate justice. She knew that to demand righteousness, she would have to demonstrate righteousness. She did not compromise her cry with corrupt conduct. Her cry was existentially calibrated to be ethically consistent. She had consecrated her cry.

That is not to say that she was not angry—I'm sure that she was. Every normal, healthy-minded human with a strong sense of right and wrong will be outraged when justice is denied. As a matter of fact, sometimes it is *right* to get angry. That is why the Ephesians 4:26 says, "Be angry and sin not: let not the sun go down upon thy wrath." When you are angry without sinning, then you can have a consecrated cry.

The media seems to be wondering why people are rioting in the wake of the jury's decision in Simi Valley. But in light of the repeated injustices that have been foisted upon the African American community, I believe that we have shown tremendous restraint. We could have rioted when the United States invaded Grenada. We could have rioted when Iraq was invaded on Martin Luther King, Jr.'s Birthday. We could have rioted when a judge let a store owner get away with the cold-blooded murder of a Black child in Los Angeles. We could have rioted many times, based on the repeated injustices that our people have experienced.

Even Jesus got angry. When he went into Jerusalem and found people buying and selling in the Temple, he did not fall on his knees and begin a prayer meeting! John says that he was so angry, so outraged, so incensed, that he made a whip out of cords and physically drove man and beast out of the Temple, turning over their tables and scattering their coins. Can you imagine some news broadcast on the order of *Nightline* covering the cleansing of the Temple?

"Today a riot erupted in the Temple Courts at the center of Jerusalem. An itinerant preacher from Galilee named Jesus and his motley group of disciples led a rampage directed at the businessmen stationed there. Property damage is now estimated at $50,000. Several moneychangers were rushed to the emergency room at General Hospital. They are now in serious, but stable condition. Jesus and his disciples are still at large, but the Roman police and the Temple guard are making every attempt to arrest him before the celebration of Passover has ended."

Consecrate your anger and channel it into righteous actions.

People will get angry. But anger is consecrated when its motive, means, and end is righteousness. When unrighteousness reigns, it is right to be angry. But in order to usher in righteousness, anger cannot melt down into emotional explosions that in themselves perpetrate their own pain and problems. Anger over injustice is never a license for vengeance. Consecrate your anger and channel it into righteous actions. It is time to stop burning down and start building up! It is time to stop criticizing and start mobilizing! It is time to stop seeking our revenge and start seeking our redemption!

Do you know that if there is *continuation* and *consecration* in your cry, it will bring *aggravation* to others? Oh yes! And that will help you get justice! You see, this woman aggravated the judge! She annoyed him. She bothered him. *She got on his nerves!* She wouldn't let him have any peace! In getting justice, you may never convert others—or even get them to change their minds to agree with you. But you will get justice! You see, this judge in Jesus' story never did change. He himself said, "Though I *still* don't fear God or care about people, I had better give this woman justice, lest she wear me out!" After the events of last week, we can see that America hasn't changed much. We have been in this hemisphere four hundred years, and all we have is four billion tears. America has changed, but it hasn't changed much. But even if they don't change, you must still cry for justice!

The late, great Reverend C. L. Franklin tells a story of a lavish banquet that was being prepared for the Queen of Peace. While the workers decked the rooms with dazzling banners and hung the glittering chandeliers, a stranger entered. The man was old, gaunt, and dressed in tattered rags. The men in the hall were taken aback at his entrance. They asked him, "What do you mean to enter our banquet hall dressed in tattered rags? Don't you know that we are expecting the Queen of Peace?" The bearded old man insisted on staying. At this they rose up in disgust, and with one accord, they pounced upon him with all of their might. With a dagger, they stabbed him to his heart. At that very time the Queen of Peace entered. She asked what the disturbance was with the man, who now lay bleeding on the floor. They told her that his presence was an affront and insult to the Queen, and that they had to remove him to properly receive her. To all of this she responded by saying. "Gentlemen, I'm sorry, but I cannot sit at your table—I cannot dine at your feast. Gentlemen, I cannot stay in this lavish banquet hall. For the old man that you have on the floor dying is Justice; and if there is no room here for Justice, then there is no room for Peace."[2]

It makes no difference what the Gross National Product of our country is. It makes no difference what the standard of living may be. It makes no difference how we bedeck the halls of our society with modern technology, innovative industry, and economic gimmickry and gadgetry. If there is no room in this country for justice, then there is certainly no room for peace.

How long will we be always suspected but never respected?

Look at what the unjust judge did—the judge that neither feared God nor cared about people. He neither feared God nor cared about people, yet he still gave justice to the widow! If the unjust judge acts thusly, do you think that God will let the people of God live in injustice if they, too, will cry out to God day and night? The logic of our faith demands an affirmative answer. The judge of all the earth will do right!

Because there is a law down here, but there is another law up there!

But for African Americans, the question remains, How long? How long will we be always suspected but never respected? How long will we be tolerated but never appreciated? How long will we be rejected and despised of men, people of sorrow and acquainted with grief?

How long? Not long! Because there are courts down here, but there is another court up there! How long? Not long! Because there is a law down here, but there is another law up there! How long? Not long! Because there is a Rodney King down here, but there is a King of kings up there! How long? Not long! Jesus is coming back!

Jesus himself is our ultimate hope for justice within history. We have more than the problem of a corrupt court. We have more than the power of a consistent cry. *We have the promise of a coming Christ!* I didn't just make that up! Jesus himself said, *"When the Son of Man comes,* will he find faith on earth?" Oh yes! Jesus is coming back! We can keep on praying! We can keep on believing! We can keep on marching! We can keep on protesting! We can keep on working for peace! We can keep on struggling for a new day! We can keep on crying out for justice! We have the promise of a coming Christ! He came before as a lamb, but he's coming back like a lion! He came before to forgive, but he's coming back to judge!

When he comes, every person will sit under their vine and fig tree, and none will be afraid! When he comes, righteousness will cover the earth as the waters cover the sea! When he comes, people will beat their swords into plowshares and their spears into pruninghooks to study war no more! When he comes, the wicked will cease from troubling! When he comes, the weary will be at rest! When he comes, every hill and mountain will be made low, every valley will be exalted, the crooked will be made straight and the rough places made smooth, and the glory of the Lord shall be revealed, and all flesh shall see it together! When he comes, there won't be problems in Simi Valley, because there will be peace in the valley! Hallelujah! Christ is coming back!

Perseverance: The Supreme Test

HENRY H. MITCHELL

Be not deceived; God is not mocked: for whatsoever a man soweth, that shall he also reap. And let us not be weary in well doing: for in due season we shall reap, if we faint not.

GALATIANS 6:7, 9

Now we come, finally, to the bottom line in all our thoughts about self-esteem: is it actually possible among oppressed people, and does it help one to persevere and stand up against the oppression? Is strong self-image among an oppressed people a figment of the psychologist's imagination, or can the oppressed actually possess real self-pride? Is self-esteem just a feel-good escape, or does it send one back into the struggle with staying power?

Obviously, escapist self-esteem is false, a desperate sort of whistling in the dark—a wanabe pride of self when I know down deep that I am not worthy of it. On the other hand, real self-esteem is too self-respecting and wholesome to stop and rest until the oppression has come to an end.

A good place to view authentic self-esteem is among some of our enslaved ancestors, who had a marvelous capacity to hold up their heads and keep opposing their oppressors. Open rebellion and covert resistance never ceased. And underneath almost all the bowing and "yessahs" to the Boss or Missie was a proud and self-respecting Black conspirator. The big question is simply, *how* did they manage to keep their pride and courage while living under such brutal and unrelenting oppression?

What seemed on the surface to be typical pie-in-the-sky piety was in fact a powerful alternative to debilitating despair.

A major aspect of the answer lay in the fact that their faith was not in themselves alone; they had a still stronger faith in God. What seemed on the surface to be typical pie-in-the-sky piety was in fact a powerful alternative to debilitating despair. First, our ancestors knew that they were somebody because they were children of God. They held onto this belief regardless of who the slave-masters said they were. Second, they knew that every dark tunnel in a believer's life had a light at the end, so it was always worth waiting until one got to the end.

The text they loved to quote in this connection was the apostle Paul's version of the Law of Identical Harvest: "Be not deceived; God is not mocked: for whatsoever persons sow, that shall they also reap. And be not weary in well doing; for in due season we shall reap if we faint not" (Gal. 6:7, 9 AP).

Their ancestors had declared the same law in many of the proverbs of African Traditional Religion. *Identical Harvest* means quite clearly that when one plants beans, one can expect only beans. The product is identical with what is planted. And, of course, the real meaning is that life works the exact same way. In the long-term rule of the Creator, love begets love, and cruelty begets cruelty. There are no exceptions. This was fully known by believing slaves to be a rule of the universe, as God made and reigns over it.

A story from the life of the noted ex-slave, abolitionist, and feminist orator Sojourner Truth illustrates how deeply slaves could hold this belief in God's Law of Identical Harvest—and how consistently their firm self-esteem could recall this law to help them endure their trials.

Early in her adult enslavement, Isabella, as Sojourner Truth was then known, had had five children taken from her and sold prior to the gradual end of slavery in New York State. Her last son, Peter, age five, fell into the hands of a New York woman and her Alabama husband, a wealthy planter named Fowler. He illegally carried the child out of the State of New York, to enslavement for life, on his plantation. He did this because the child would have been set free at age twenty-one in New York.

Still young in the Christian faith, Isabella found meaning for life amidst this absurd cruelty by calling on the sure and certain justice of the Judge of all the Earth. For her, God just simply is not mocked. No race is exempt, and no class is rich enough to circum-vent the long arm of God's justice. To assume that it could be otherwise would be a mockery of the Maker. And regardless of who it may be, *nobody* mocks the Maker. One way or the other, the justice of God will guarantee returns exactly like what one plants in the fields of life.

And, furthermore, by implication, cruel masters just don't get away with mocking God's sincere servants. Their worth as *persons* in the sight of God is guaranteed in the processes of justice. There was, however, an important qualification to this Law of Identical Harvest that so wonderfully guaranteed respect of persons. One had to wait for the "due season" of which Paul wrote in Galatians 6:9. It was a well known fact that seeds sprout and grow, and plants bear their fruit according to their own schedule, not ours. The justice of the Judge of all the Earth was not to be seen at will, and no human being had the right to hold a stopwatch on God.

This part of the law of identical harvest called for patience on the part of the oppressed. Due season gave the believing slave a way to understand and deal with the most discouraging of immediate prospects. Here the true measure of our ancestors' self-esteem is once again evident. Slaves *had* to believe that they really were the children of God, to whom they were important. Without this faith they could not have trusted so deeply that brutal slave masters, regardless of all their supposed power, were still not in charge. God was.

Thus what was often mistaken for ignorant contentment on the part of the enslaved was in fact deep faith in the Creator, whose time frame is infinitely longer than ours. The proper respect due believing slaves was not often enforced from heaven right on the spot. But not to worry; our ancestors knew that in due season, masters reap what they sow just like everybody else. Belief in the due season of God gave great patience, and monumental perseverance to the oppressed.

Isabella marvelously illustrated this characteristic of perseverance in her efforts to recover her son Peter from enslavement in Alabama.

When she first heard of the removal of her son to Alabama, she set out immediately to confront her former master, Dumont, and, hopefully, to have him jailed for breaking the law. Her first encounter was with Mrs. Dumont, who scoffed at the very idea of the child even belonging to its mother, as opposed to the master. She also made fun of Isabella's limited resources. The slow, solemn, insistent reply was, "I'll have my child again." As for having no money to get or take care of little Peter, Isabella unflinchingly declared, "No, I have no money, but God has enough." The most insulting of rejoinders by her former mistress made neither a dent in her faith nor, as a result, in her dogged determination.

It turned out that the real culprit was the person to whom Dumont had sold the child. His name was Gedney, and he in turn had handed the child over to his son-in-law, Fowler. Again, Isabella confronted the wife, who was also the mother of Mrs. Fowler. Again the master's wife thought it comical that Isabella should have the nerve to demand the cancellation of the sale and the return of her son. Mrs. Gedney's laugh seemed almost demonic. It was a crushing defeat.

But Isabella kept praying and trusting, and soon she met a man who was disposed to help her. He directed her to some Quakers who, he confided, were already indignant about the illegal sale of her son. These Quakers helped and went well beyond. They almost caused a crisis for Isabella, because they assigned her a room with a bed, and she had never slept on anything but the floor. Their kindness continued, and they carried her to Kingston, and directed her to the court house, where she was to file a complaint with the grand jury.

That sounds simple enough, but poor Isabella had no idea what a grand jury was, and went through several mistaken efforts to get tall (grand) men to serve as jurors. It was embarrassing, and one could easily have given up. But her faith gave her perseverance, and eventually she went through the right door and asked to present her case to the sitting grand jury.

It seemed too good to be true when the grand jury agreed to hear her case. But there were still other obstacles. She was laughed at when she didn't know what to do with the Bible used for her swearing in. She didn't understand the technicalities required. But even with all of this, she still did get the writ. She was directed to carry it to New Paltz, New York, and have it served on Solomon Gedney, the man who had sold her son Peter to his son-in-law, Fowler of Alabama.

But the obstacles continued. Gedney avoided service of the writ. But he did get smart sound legal advice and eventually went to Alabama to retrieve the child. This all took the better part of a year, while Gedney first hid from the law and then took the slowest boats and trains available. When he returned to New York, he kept Peter in his possession as a slave, and assumed he had avoided or reversed his standing as a lawbreaker. All this time Isabella was forced to wonder when it would all end, but she never gave up.

When she learned that Peter was back in Gedney's hands, she once again sought legal counsel. The lawyer had the writ served on Gedney, who posted bond and agreed to appear in court. But now came another obstacle. The court didn't sit again for months. The lawyer's comfort to her now was that if Gedney disposed of the child in the meantime, she would get half of the $600 posted as bond. Isabella put her hands on her hips and let the lawyer know that she wasn't after money, and that she not only was going to have her son back; she was going to do so *before* the court finally reconvened. She didn't have the slightest notion how all this was going to happen, but she was convinced it would happen. So still trusting, she simply went back to work one more time.

Then a new problem arose. Isabella clearly sensed that the folks who had been helping her had more patience with this prolonged process than she, and they were losing their patience with her impatience. It may have seemed to some like outright ingratitude. Not knowing any further step she could take, she prayed constantly, and wondered and waited in hope for God to direct her.

She soon came upon a complete stranger in the street, who, without even exchanging names, walked up to her and wanted to know if she had got her boy back. When she said she hadn't, he advised, "Do you see that house yonder? Well, Lawyer Demain lives there. Go to him and lay your case before him; I think he'll help you. *Stick to him.* Don't give him peace till he does. I feel sure if you press him, he'll do it for you."

He didn't have to convince Isabella, and he did not have to explain it twice. She sprang to the task immediately. Lawyer Demain heard her story and thought a while. He then offered one more obstacle. If she would bring him five dollars fetching charge, he would have her son brought to her in twenty-four hours. She ran to some Quaker friends ten miles away and raised the five dollars. Then, knowing no clock or watch, she went through the longest twenty-four hours of her life. She became a nuisance, until the lawyer promised to notify her on her boy's arrival.

When Gedney and the boy, Peter, finally did come, they had to appear before a justice who, surprisingly, faced one odd and final complication. Peter didn't even recognize his mother. He pleaded to be allowed to remain with his master, who had fully scared and prepared the boy for the hearing. The justice wisely interpreted the situation, and Isabella was at last given her son, who soon recalled, "Well you do look like my mother used to look."

For the ecstatically joyous Isabella, her endurance and perseverance had been justified. Her belief that she and her family were important as God's children, and her certainty that all people reap in due season what they have sowed, had been strengthened all the more.

Because of her amazing faith in justice and her forgiving spirit, there is one final twist to this story. Moved by a serious illness in their family, Isabella consented to serve a brother of the senior Gedneys, of all people! This man had mercilessly and falsely vilified her in court, but even so she answered the call for help. She had been in his house hardly two hours when word came that Fowler in Alabama had brutally murdered his wife, who was the Gedneys' daughter! He was in jail awaiting trial.

This could have been a great moment of triumphant, vengeful delight for Isabella, but once again she responded in deep faith and prayed for guidance in the crisis.

Isabella remembered how astonished and heartsick she had been when she saw on her son the evidences of brutal kickings and beatings from head to foot. She had prayed, "Oh, Lord, render unto them double!" She later reported, "I dared not find fault with God, exactly; but the language of my heart was, 'Oh, my God! that's too much—I did not mean quite so much, God.' " What a faith! And what compassion one has to have to feel like this about the justice of God applied to one's heartless oppressors.

But God's apparent "repayment in full" was even worse than this murder. The same mistress (Mrs. Gedney) who had cruelly ridiculed Isabella for mourning the loss of her enslaved child now lost her very sanity over her own daughter's death. Isabella was deeply awed at both the providence of God, which had placed her in the path of this news, and at the justice of God, which had struck so fiercely to punish her persecutors. It was an awesomely empowering affirmation of oneself, to see so many forces brought to bear on her behalf, as it seemed. If all this was done for her, she must surely be God's child! Somebody ought to see it and be warned: "Never mess with God's children! You pay dearly when you mistreat believers like Isabella!"[3]

Yet this interpretation of God's movement of things on her behalf was never accepted boastfully or in joy at her enemies' downfall. It did reinforce her faith-begotten determination to persevere, and her solid self-esteem. One hears it in Isabella's unforgettable reaction to the insulting discouragement of Mrs. Dumont, her former mistress, who thought it ridiculous to make such a fuss over "losing a little nigger." On that occasion, not only did Isabella solemnly and confidently declare, "I'll have my child again!" She also later reported the course of her inner thoughts at that time: "Oh my God! I know'd I'd have him agin. I was sure God would help me to get him. Why I felt so tall within—I felt as if the power of a nation was within me." My God! My God! What great faith!

With a faith like this,
    we'll never get tired of tryin' to do right,
    we'll never get too fatigued to fight for justice,
    we'll never give up in the face of multiplied obstacles.

Oh be not weary in well doing, for I declare unto you, harvest time is coming, and in due season we shall reap,

we shall all reap.

we shall all reap bountifully,

pressed down and running over.

We can't help feeling good about how God backs us up and lets nobody do us wrong without punishment.

And so we sing with joy,

If anybody asks you who I am,

who I am, who I am,

If anybody asks you who I am,

Tell 'em I'm a child of God![4]

Questions for Discussion

The Cry for Justice

1. If you could have just one request from American society, which would it be? Much money, high political office, equal justice, or equal education? Why?

2. How do you react to Martin Luther King, Jr.'s early opinion that justice can be gained by appealing to the majority conscience? How does this compare with the judge in the story?

3. What do you think of nuisance tactics to gain rights already granted by the Constitution? How does this differ from repeated pleas as a way to get things from your parents?

4. Do you think there are ever public positions in the USA where African Americans can feel secure on their own merits? Why?

5. Is it better to suffer injustice in silence, showing strength, or to cry out constantly? Is there a place for both? Explain.

Perseverance: The Supreme Test

1. What do you think of questioning God about why oppression prospers and sinners flourish? Does God resent questions? Explain.
2. Describe somebody you know who is calm in the face of discrimination. Did her or his cool stop efforts against injustice? Was he or she just cool, calm, and self-confident? Explain.
3. Suppose bigotry and cruel oppression went unpunished in the world. If God were not just, would anybody else need to be? Could anybody, of any race, feel valuable? Why?
4. List all the reasons you can think of for giving up, and for going on in the struggle against oppression.

CHAPTER 9

Preaching for
Black Self-Esteem

*We are black, not because we are cursed, for blackness is not a curse;
it is a curse only if you think so, and, you know, it's not really a curse
then; it's just the way you think. . . . All colors are beautiful in the sight
of God. . . . And the only reason you entertain a thought like that is
because you have been culturally conditioned by white people to think
that way, and they conditioned you that way because they used this as
a means to an end, to give you a feeling of inferiority, and to then take
advantage of you, socially, economically, and politically.*[1]

elf-esteem occurs when (1) people receive more information about themselves, and (2) people begin to
celebrate appropriately their God-given worth. Biblical preaching in the tradition of the African American
church is an appropriate context in which to share this information, as well as the appropriate catalyst to begin this celebration.
The preaching tradition of the African American church has
always been a primary source of information and inspiration that
gives Black people a sacred sense of who they are and whose they
are. For Black people to maintain their psychic health and spiritual
wholeness, this tradition must continue to survive and thrive.

In chapter 1, the need for ethnic self-esteem was established
with a history of the identity crisis in Black America and a
presentation of symptoms of low ethnic self-esteem. These symp-

toms were grouped in five axes: (1) Black caste, (2) Black characteristics, (3) the Black continent, (4) Black capacity, and (5) Black culture. Each axis represents a pastoral problem with prophetic implications. A primary method of ministering to these needs in individuals and the community is through the healing infomation and inspiration of biblical preaching.

Chapter 2 presented a history and theology of Black self-esteem. Tracing the affirmation of ethnic identity from African Traditional Religions to African American Christianity, the tradition of a ministry of healing and wholeness was established. Also, a scripture-based theology of self-esteem was set forth, rooted primarily in the Love Ethic of Jesus, as stipulated in passages such as Mark 12:29-31.

Chapters 3 through 7 give examples of a preaching ministry that targets areas of low ethnic self-esteem, with each chapter providing two sermons addressing a Black self-esteem need from the perspectives of two preachers. Chapter 3 addresses the issue of the Black caste; that of being born into an ethnic group that has historically been oppressed as the degraded other. "Don't Count Me Out" handles the issue of social rejection, while "Bethlehem Revisited" highlights our God-given resources for transcendence. Chapter 4 confronts the aesthetics of Black characteristics with sermons expressing the need to learn to love our own looks. "The Skin I'm In" provides a biblically based rationale for the acceptance of one's color, while "God's Handiwork: Me!" speaks of a Creator who sculpts ethnic features with artistic excellence. Chapter 5 wrestles with African American ambivalence toward Africa, the Black Continent. "The Drama of a Daddy with a Dream" reflects upon the presence of Jesus in Africa, and "The Roots of the Spirit" connects Black American fruit with its African root. Chapter 6 deals with Black capacity, which has been berated by racist notions of inferiority and inadequacy. "The Cornerstone Conspiracy" notes that Christ's capacity was also challenged, and "Wisdom Redefined" identifies uncelebrated gifts in Black people that have empowered many for survival and success. Chapter 7 is a celebration of Black Culture. "Buppies in the Palace" discusses how to utilize one's culture even after "arriving" in the dominant society, and "Epistle to the Young, Gifted and Black" lifts up Timothy's unique gifts of bicultural participation.

Chapter 8 is not based upon a need for ethnic self-esteem but seeks to speak to the social structures that impose a state of oppressed existence upon African Americans. "The Cry for Justice" was a sermon preached to a Black congregation in California the Sunday following the Los Angeles uprising of 1992. "Perseverance: The Supreme Test" provides biblical insights into the Black theology of survival. This chapter is an acknowledgment that low ethnic self-esteem cannot be properly seen outside of its social, political, and economic context.

This book has resulted from a labor to maintain a laserlike focus on preaching as a ministry to enhance the ethnic self-esteem of African Americans. However, it is hoped that the particularity of focus will bear universal results. As the microcosm is often the best starting point to perceive the macrocosm, insights into the struggle of Black people may yield information that can aid both the identity crises and liberation struggles of other peoples. The twentieth century has proven that Black liberation movements have provided patterns and paradigms for similar quests for justice. If the self-esteem syllogism of chapter 4 is true, then all of God's peoples are beautiful—be they identified as African, Native American, Asian, European, or whatever! The beauty of humanity is in its rich diversity! Appreciation of unique ethnicities should lead to celebration of the entire human family, and usher forth in glorification of God! Through this kind of preaching, the liberating ministry of Jesus Christ is extended.

"The Spirit of the Lord is on me,
　because God has anointed me
　to preach good news to the poor.
He has sent me to proclaim freedom for the prisoners
　and recovery of sight for the blind,
to release the oppressed,
　to proclaim the year of the Lord's favor." (Luke 4:18-19 NIV)

Notes

1. Black Self-Esteem: A Vital Need in Search of a Vibrant Ministry

1. Frantz Fanon, *Black Skin, White Masks* (New York: Grove Press, 1967), p. 63.
2. W. E. B. DuBois, *The Souls of Black Folk* (New York: Vintage Books, 1991), pp. 8-9.
3. The science of modern anthropology identifies all humans as being of one race, or species. *Race* as a term for different nationalites or physical types emerged as a psuedo-scientific explanation for notions of White superiority and serve as justifications of European imperialism. Here we will use the term *race* in its colloquial sense. For a rational discussion of race from a modern anthropological perspective, see Ashley Montagu's *The Prevalence of Nonsense* (New York: Harper & Row, 1967), chap. 5, "Absurdities About Race," pp. 126-50. See also Cornel West's *Prophesy Deliverance!* (Philadelphia: Westminster Press, 1982), pp. 47-57 for a brilliant "Genealogy of Modern Racism."
4. Stanley Coopersmith, *The Antecedents of Self-Esteem* (San Francisco: W. H. Freeman & Co., 1967), pp. 4-5.
5. Ibid., p. 38.
6. James H. Cone, *Black Theology and Black Power* (New York: Seabury Press, 1969), p. 11.

3. Self-Esteem and Black Caste: Conditions of Birth

1. James Weldon Johnson, *The Autobiography of an Ex-Coloured Man* (New York: Vintage Books, 1989), pp. 17-18.

4. Self-Esteem and Black Characteristics: Loving the Way We Look

1. Bishop Henry McNeil Turner, "God Is a Negro," in John Bracy, August Meir, and Elliot Rudwick, eds., *Black Nationalism in America* (Indianapolis and New York: Bobbs-Merrill, 1970), p. 154.

2. Rance Allen, "Miracle Worker," Alvert Music Co., Stora Music Co., Roxatlanta Lane Music Co. (BMI), 1991

5. Self-Esteem and the Black Continent

1. Countee Cullen, "Heritage," in *Dark Symphony: Negro Literature in America*, James Emmanuel and Theodore Gross, eds. (New York: Macmillan, 1968), pp. 176-79.

6. Self-Esteem and Black Capacity

1. Robert H. Hill and Barbara Blair, eds., *Marcus Garvey: Life and Lessons* (Berkeley: University of California Press, 1987), p. 45.
2. Edward Mote, "My Hope Is Built" in *The United Methodist Hymnal* (Nashville: The United Methodist Publishing House, 1989), no. 368.

7. Self-Esteem and Black Culture

1. Cheikh Anta Diop, *Civilization or Barbarism: An Authentic Anthropology* (Brooklyn: Lawrence Hill Books, 1991), p. 211
2. A. Bazel Androzzo, "If I Can Help Somebody," M.C.A. Publishing Co., 1945.
3. Traditional African American song of praise.

8. Self-Esteem and Oppressed Existence

1. Toni Morrison, *Sula* (New York: Penguin Books, 1982), p. 90.
2. C. L. Franklin, "What Think Ye of Jesus?" (Chess Sermon no. 24). Copyright © Chess Records, Englewood, N.J., 1977.
3. This account of Sojourner Truth's experiences is adapted from *Sojourner Truth: Narrative and Book of Life* (Chicago: Johnson Publishing Co., 1970), pp. 14-41.
4. Traditional African American spiritual.

9. Preaching for Black Self-Esteem

1. C. L. Franklin "The Preacher Who Got Drunk" in Jeff Todd Tilt, ed., *Give Me This Mountain* (Chicago: University of Illinois Press, 1989), pp. 186-87.